The
FOCALGUIDE
to
Movie
Titling

THE ⓕ FOCALGUIDES TO

The FOCALGUIDE to Movie Titling

Philip Jenkins

Focal Press Limited, London

Focal Press Inc., New York

🔲 British Library Cataloguing in Publication Data

Jenkins, Philip
    Focal guide to movie titling. – (Focal guides).
    1. Moving-pictures – Titling
    I. Title   II. Series
    778.5'35   TR899

ISBN 0 240 51011 9

American Library of Congress Catalog No.

80-40788

FOCAL PRESS LTD.,
31 Fitzroy Square, London. W1P 6BH

FOCAL PRESS INC.,
10 East 40th Street, New York, NY 10016

Associated companies:
Pitman Publishing Pty Ltd., Melbourne.
Pitman Publishing New Zealand Ltd., Wellington.

Printed in Great Britain by Thomson Litho Ltd, East Kilbride and bound by Hunter & Foulis Ltd, Edinburgh

Contents

Introduction

You need make only the simplest 'start' and 'end' titles for your reel of film, but immediately the film takes on a professionalism, a completeness, that stamps you as a true movie-maker, rather than just another person with a movie camera. The difference is amazing: a title at the start of each film, and one at the end adds a degree of 'finish' to even the simplest home movie. Everyone expects an introductory title, announcing what is about to be seen, and an end title to bring the film positively to a close. However, most people with a movie camera have never made a title in their lives. They think it is difficult, and have never been shown how easy it can be, and how satisfying it is to create really effective titles.

You do not need sunshine to film titles—though you can use it for the lighting. It is easier to use simple indoor lighting. You do not need a lot of lights because the title area is usually relatively small and easily lit with one or two bulbs.

Most titles are formal, and can be made by setting out plastic letters, making a title card with transfer-type lettering, using a typewriter or, if you have some creative talent drawing your own title card. Whatever you do you will find great scope for ingenuity and for developing flair, in the use of coloured backgrounds, for example. In this book is the essential know-how about using all types of movie cameras, for shooting titles. Included also are the simple rules for layout, letter sizes and style, and practical hints on using the types of relatively inexpensive lettering available on the market. Then there is the fascinating aspect of tricks in titling, animated titles, reverse action, rolls and scrolls, and superimpositions. Fades and dissolves are especially valuable in titles, and when to use them and how to makes these effects are explained. With these highly practical guidelines, you will find titling great fun giving tremendous scope for your imagination and ingenuity.

Titles are Everywhere

The simplest way to make titles is to shoot those that occur naturally. When you look around you will see many useful examples that might have escaped your notice. Notice boards and place names for example, are natural title material. When you see a subject of this sort immediately consider whether it would make a good title. Then think how best to shoot it so that it *looks* like a title.

Place-name boards

On your travels you may see a sign such as: *Welcome to Yellow-stone National Park.* Here, obviously, is potential title material. You might plan to use it as a subtitle to introduce a sequence of the park. Possibly you might use it as a main title if the park is the only subject of your film. Again, you might start with a formal title: *Our holiday in the West,* and follow this with a natural title of a huge illuminated sign: *Welcome to Weston-Super-Mare.*

How to shoot it

Consider the wording on the sign or notice board as a title and decide how best you can shoot it to add the touch of formality that a title—particularly a main title—demands. First, if you can use a fade-in to start the shot, you will find it much more effective as a title. Second, use 'tight' framing, so that little else is included other than the name or notice that forms your wording.

The formal fade-in is one of the best openings to use. At the other end of the shot the transition from the natural title to the following shot offers many interesting possibilities. You may, for example, use a zoom-out from the tightly framed wording all the way to wide-angle, so the shot then shows the entire surroundings. This sets the scene. Another way is to combine a zoom-out with a pan to a general view of the location. In this way you will simulate the natural process of the eye, looking from place to place in the scene. If your camera allows it, you can use a dissolve from your title shot to the surrounding general view. This can be most effective giving a very smooth transition from the title to the picture.

Adding your own lettering

Not all natural titles are readymade. You may have to do part of the work yourself. On the beach it is a simple matter to write a title in the sand using a stick. The letters can be large or small depending on the distance from which you plan to shoot them, and the focal length of your camera lens. A zoom gives quite a bit of latitude in this respect. You might film the letters in the sand from a high viewpoint by shooting from up on the sea-front. A variation on this is to do the title by the water's edge, and let the sea flow over the wording to obliterate it. This is particularly effective with an end title when it would logically be followed by a fade-out. When using the sea to obliterate the wording you may need to shoot the title in two stages, with the camera firmly on its tripod and not moved during the shot. You film the words while the sea is safely some distance away, then stop the camera, wait for the sea to get near and continue shooting as the first wave sweeps into the picture and over the lettering.

Before starting to shoot a natural title, consider how it will fit into the film, how it will start, how long to hold it (always slightly longer than it takes to read it), and how it will end—eg: fade, dissolve, zoom-out, pan, or just a simple cut. Balance the inherent informality of most 'natural' titles with the need for a certain amount of formality. It is *announcing* something and you want your audience to take special note of it. The natural title has the advantage of giving the atmosphere of the film and of helping to set the scene.

Rock-steady titles

It is essential for any title to be absolutely rock-steady on the screen. The only way to achieve this is to have the camera on a

How to use natural titles. For a place-name board in a natural location, start with a wide-angle shot of the whole scene, then zoom in to a close-up of the name board. It is worth taking the trouble to find a dramatic viewpoint. The Paris road sign, for example, has a dynamic diagonal composition which powerfully suggests forward movement. In the St Louis title, the railway line effectively underlines the name board.

tripod or other firm support. Never compromise on this; take the trouble to use the tripod for any shot destined for use as a title. It has been rightly said of all filming that the first rule for achieving professional looking results is always to use a tripod. It is especially important with titles. Unsteady wording on the screen is like reading a newspaper that is being jiggled up and down. The convention is that wording must be static so that it can be read more easily. This applies as much to movies as to the printed page. There is, though, the interesting question of whether some movement might be permissible within the scene so long as the wording —for example, a notice board—is static. The answer is that slight movement in the surroundings is often *desirable.* It can make just that difference between a movie—which by definition can move— and a still slide, which cannot. Movement within the picture must, however, be unobtrusive. For example, a name-board might be framed by a convenient tree-branch with its leaves gently swaying in the breeze. This would be quite acceptable: it is not detracting from the reading of the wording, and is perfectly natural. Indeed, only in a still-picture slide would the leaves *not* move a little.

It is natural for film to show movement. Later we consider the way to add artificial 'movement' when filming still-picture slides for titles and inserts. But what you must always avoid is movement that draws the eye away from the principal subject: the wording you want your audience to read. A seaside place-name sign could have seagulls wheeling around in the sky over the lettering. The words you want your audience to read would, however, be very much bolder and quite still on the screen.

Carry a set of plastic letters'

Finally, there is the do-it-yourself-on-location title. By carrying a box of plastic letters with you—preferably moderately large ones—you are all set to lay out the lettering and shoot an appropriate title there and then. This is a really rewarding way to make titles. It has the advantage that the title background exactly matches the scene, and the titles are ready at the same time as the rest of the film is received back from processing.

The easiest way to shoot laid-out lettering is to use a tripod that will aim down towards the ground—not necessarily vertically, but usually so. You can know your photographed area at the nearest focusing distance by spending a few moments looking into the viewfinder at the measured distance. You then set the lettering out so that it will be a reasonable size on the screen when you have filmed it.

It is a good idea to have different sizes of letters to cover different eventualities and, in some situations, self-adhesive letters (p 44) can be used. Remember that if you stick these letters on to a rough or dusty surface you will spoil the adhesive for future use. You can, however, wipe off all the ineffective adhesive with solvent, then apply more from a special refill tube.

One of the most effective uses of 'natural' titles is the simple superimposed title made by sticking self-adhesive letters on a sheet of glass which is then supported perfectly still in front of the camera, with the background scene visible beyond the lettering. The whole world of title-making is open to imaginative treatment—but the object is always to use words to convey the required information as smoothly and as appropriately as possible. This is the art of title-making.

Using your Camera for Titling

You can use virtually any movie camera for shooting titles from the simplest non-zoom camera, to the most elaborate reflex zoom. Provided you know how, they can all be used.

Some cameras are more convenient than others, however, because most titles are filmed with title cards which are smaller in area than even the close-up subjects for which many cameras are designed. So you need to use the simpler cameras, closer to the title than the normal nearest focusing distance. This is achieved by fitting a supplementary lens to the front of your camera lens.

How close?

Most of the cameras being made today are zoom lens models, and almost all of them have a focusing adjustment on the lens. Most zoom lens cameras will focus down to 1.5 m (5 ft), though some will go down to about 1.2 m (4 ft). Most useful of all for titling are those which have lenses focusing down to 1 m (3.3 ft) or even to 0.9 m (3 ft).

In general, the longer the zoom range of the lens, the smaller the area it is capable of covering at its nearest focusing distance. For example, a typical 8:1 zoom that focuses down to 3 ft will take in a subject width of only about 90 mm or $3\frac{1}{2}$ in. This specification is ideal for titling and makes it particularly easy, for you can set the camera at the minimum distance and then use the zoom to control the width of subject taken in.

The zooming range of the lens, that is, the ratio of the shortest focal length to the longest, tells you the range of title widths you can take in without moving the camera. Thus, if your camera takes in, say, $3\frac{1}{2}$ in at the telephoto end of a zoom of 8:1 range, the wide-angle end will take in eight times as much, namely a 28 in wide subject. And, of course, you can set the zoom anywhere in the range. Not surprisingly, perhaps, only the more dedicated enthusiasts will have such equipment, and for the most modest cameras the addition of a 'No 2' supplementary lens (usually +2 dioptres 'strength') will enable the camera to be used at a distance of approximately $19\frac{1}{2}$ in and to take in a convenient width of title for most work.

Focusing distance

When discussing camera distance, remember that all cine lenses and cameras today are scaled in distance from the film-plane. This is generally indicated on the camera by a vertical line through a small circle, thus: ϕ. If you add a supplementary lens, you should generally put the lens' focus to its infinity setting, and measure the distance from the supplementary (p 27).

An exception to this latter rule is when the manufacturer of a camera supplies a special supplementary, and quotes distances specifically from the film-plane.

Reflex viewfinder

The most useful feature of a movie camera for titling is undoubtedly a reflex viewfinder. This allows you to view the subject through the actual taking lens. Thus you can clearly see what you will be taking in a sharp-edged frame. This is invaluable when lining up titles.

Remember, however, that on any reflex camera when you look into the viewfinder you are not looking at the film-gate itself. You are in fact looking at a rather small frame, set up by the manufacturer as closely as possible to match what you will later see on the screen when you project the film. In the camera you are not even looking at the equivalent of the film-gate aperture, which is always slightly larger than the projector gate, to avoid cut-off edges on the screen. Most reflex viewfinders, even on high-price movie cameras, are not quite accurate. This is something you may never notice with ordinary subjects. But titles generally need fairly accurate lining up because some of them have to be centred, and you must never show the edges of the title card in the picture.

So for critical work you are well advised to test the viewfinder accuracy on your particular camera. This is simple to do (p. 63).

Title size

The size (or sizes) of titles you can conveniently film will be determined by your particular camera and any supplementary lens you may choose, and these, of course, determine the approximate size of your title card. From this, you will see that the size of lettering is also largely determined on how many words are in the title. Obviously you would not use typewritten lettering for a title card around 8 or 10 in across; the lettering would be too small to be legible on the screen. Equally, you would not use 20 mm ($\frac{3}{4}$ in) high plastic letters if you have a camera that lets you take titles only a couple of inches across. The smallest letter size is related to the width and height of your photographed area (p. 25).

Non-reflex cameras

A great many users have non-reflex cameras—in particular some perfectly efficient 16 mm models which have a simple viewfinder 'spy-tube' system alongside the taking lens but separated from it. Here, on close-up filming such as titling, when you look through the viewfinder you see a view that is different from the one seen by the taking lens itself. Some of these simple finder systems have an adjustment that swings the viewfinder tube inwards for closer distances, but the less complex non-reflex cameras do not even have this adjustment. Instead you have to make allowance for the different views of finder and taking lens, as well as for the inherent inaccuracy, or at least vagueness, of this type of finder system. Clearly the non-reflex camera can never be as useful and flexible for titling as a through-the-lens reflex model, but here is a guide to making the necessary adjustments.

Suppose your viewfinder tube is 25 mm (1 in) to the side of your taking lens. As a rough approximation in this case, you could say that the centre of the filmed area will be just about 25 mm (1 in) sideways from the viewfinder image centre. You can allow for this by making a simple template (p. 68).

Most non-reflex viewfinders are the relatively simple 'reverse Galilean' design (opera glasses in reverse). With this system, unfortunately, you do not see the edges of the frame as sharp. Thus the picture limits become rather a matter of conjecture— particularly if you move the position of your eye and thus change the view. Many of these simple viewfinders have a built-in safety factor to help the novice avoid cutting off important parts of the subject. This, too, must be allowed for when framing a title in the viewfinder. For titling purposes, this sort of vagueness, is not good enough, and the best thing is to calculate the theoretical title area that will be photographed rather than to shoot a test. This can be done on the end of a roll of other subjects.

Thereafter, with a non-reflex camera, it is most convenient to use a fixed set-up that allows you to replace the camera in accurate location to a standardized size of title (p. 68).

Zoom reflex cameras

The owner of a camera with through-the-lens viewing is not limited to one fixed set-up, since the reflex viewfinder can be used for lining up afresh at any time. You can, of course, make allowances for the slight but almost inevitable inaccuracies of your particular viewfinder, since these are relatively small and easily taken into account.

Focusing

Remember that a reflex viewfinder does not necessarily give accurate visual focusing. Many of the simpler zoom reflex cameras have only an aerial-image viewfinder and this will not permit accurate focusing by eye. The reason is that the image you see in the viewfinder is focused 'in space', as it were, in the plane of the frame that defines the edges of the picture, and on which the eyepiece should be focused. But your eye will have no difficulty in accommodating itself on to the plane of the image in the view-finder. And if that image plane moves to or fro, as it does when the focusing is incorrect, then the viewfinder image will still look sharply focused, even if the main image is not sharp upon the film in the gate.

To avoid – or at least minimize – these problems, most of the better cameras have a focusing aid, either a microprism or split-image rangefinder, sometimes a ground glass screen, or even simple crosswires in the viewfinder image plane. Any of these will help to define the correct focus plane to the eye looking into the viewfinder. That these various visual focusing aids are generally less accurate than one might wish, is largely due to the extremely small frame-size of movie film, particularly 8 mm and Super 8. With these gauges, the magnification on projection is typically around 200-times, yet in the camera one is trying to focus accurately on a viewfinder image usually around the actual frame size – less than $\frac{1}{4}$ in (6 mm) wide on Super 8, for example. Even with a reasonably high magnification eyepiece, of perhaps around 10-times or a little more, to achieve sufficient accuracy on focusing visually is asking a lot.

The significant point about titling is that much of the filming is relatively close up, and is almost always indoors by artificial light. Therefore you tend to need large lens apertures and hence have rather little depth of field. The practical answer for titling is to set the focus as closely as you can, by measurement if possible, or at least with as careful visual focusing as can be achieved. Then you should obtain as much depth as you can by using plenty of light, and hence a correspondingly small working aperture on the lens.

Macro facilities

Particularly if you have a camera with *macro-focusing*, of the type that relies completely on visual focusing, you should be sure to use plenty of light for the filming, and therefore a small working aperture. The special point about macro-focusing is that on many lenses this is achieved by setting the zoom to its *widest* angle, and then decoupling the zooming components and using one of these alone to achieve close-up focusing by moving the zooming ring.

For this macro mode, then, the lens may be at its wide-angle end of the zoom range, where it is, in any case, inherently difficult to focus accurately. Depth of field—that is, in the subject plane—may be large, but depth of focus (*image* plane) is extremely small. So, if you use the macro as your means of close-up focusing for titles, you can only do your best and use plenty of light so that the lens will be reasonably well stopped down for more depth.

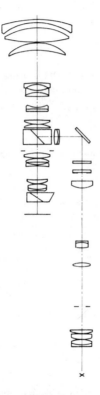

Typical zoom lens with reflex viewfinder system. A beamsplitter prism with semi-silvered reflecting face divides off a proportion of the light the lens, reflecting it to the viewfinder system. The remainder of the light passes through the prism block, lens iris the image-forming prime lens section of the zoom, and on to the film-gate. A second beamsplitter prism, reflects another small proportion of on-axis light to a CdS cell (not shown) for automatic exposure metering.

Basic Rules of Titling

The secret of making titles that look good, is to follow a few simple but very basic rules.

Format shape

The first thing you must know is the proportions for the cine frame. This is 4:3, or as the mathematically inclined professionals call it, 1.33:1. The 4:3 format applies to all the cine gauges, whether Super 8, Single-8, standard 8 mm, or 16 mm. It also applies to professional 35 mm of standard format, though this is rarely used nowadays in professional projection where 'widescreen' is now the norm.

However, virtually all amateur film is shot in 4:3 format. This means you can work within a title area of, for example, 4×3 in, $6 \times 4\frac{1}{2}$ in, 8×6 in, 12×9 in or, smaller, $2 \times 1\frac{1}{2}$ in, all of which maintain the standard 4:3 format. Obviously you can use metric sizes if preferred, for example, 24×18 cm, 16×12 cm, and so on.

Title size

Two factors determine a convenient size of title. First, how small an area is it technically possible to focus upon with your particular camera? Second, with which letter size is it convenient to work? Obviously the two factors are inter-related.

The greater the flexibility of your camera in filming down to small widths of title original, the more choice you have in title size and letter size. Happily, the majority of cameras likely to be used for title-making today are zoom reflex types. These give considerable flexibility because they can be set readily in focus over a range of title widths.

If you have a camera fitted with a focusing zoom lens, the limiting factor will be how close will it focus, and then at full zoom (ie telephoto) the width of the area filmed. You can check this in moments by setting your camera on a tripod at the appropriate distance, putting a ruler across the field of view, and checking the width seen in the viewfinder. In practice, you will generally allow a fraction more than this, to allow for viewfinder characteristics (p. 60). By using the zoom, you can include greater widths, of course, and this is highly convenient.

If you have a fixed-lens, non-reflex camera, you will have to add a supplementary lens over the camera lens, in order to focus close enough. This will greatly limit you, probably to one title width, for convenience. Indeed, you can standardize on a particular set-up and make all your title cards to suit it.

Reflex zoom cameras that will not focus close enough can still be used by adding a supplementary lens. For optical correction reasons it is generally not desirable to use very strong (ie: short focus) supplementaries for very close filming, but the usual +1 or +2 dioptre supplementaries are quite practical, and avoid having to use excessively long camera-to-title distances.

Supplementary lenses

With many modern zoom reflex cameras, you will be able to photograph sufficiently small title cards without needing any additional equipment. Indeed, cameras having a non-interchangeable, focusing lens will also focus down to short distances. With non-focusing cameras, you obviously have no choice but to use a supplementary in front of the camera lens.

The basic rule for using supplementaries is that you set the camera lens to infinity, and the *distance from supplementary to film-plane* equals the focal length of the supplementary.

Normally, supplementary lenses have their power expressed not in focal length, but in dioptres. This is simply the inverse of the focal length in metres. For example, a lens of 1 m (39.37 in) has a power of 1-dioptre. Or a lens of $\frac{1}{2}$ m focal length has a power of 2-dioptres, and so on. The table on p. 26 gives the conversion information in convenient form.

CONVERSION OF DIOPTRES TO INCHES AND CENTIMETRES

Power in dioptres	$\frac{1}{4}$	$\frac{1}{2}$	$\frac{3}{4}$	1	$1\frac{1}{2}$	2	$2\frac{1}{2}$
Focus in centimetres	400	200	133.3	100	66.67	50.0	40.0
Focus in inches	$157\frac{1}{2}$	$78\frac{3}{4}$	$52\frac{1}{2}$	$39\frac{5}{8}$	$26\frac{1}{4}$	$19\frac{11}{16}$	$15\frac{3}{4}$

Power in dioptres	3	$3\frac{1}{2}$	4	$4\frac{1}{2}$	5	$5\frac{1}{2}$	6
Focus in centimetres	33.33	28.58	25.0	22.22	20.0	18.20	16.67
Focus in inches	$13\frac{1}{2}$	$11\frac{1}{4}$	$9\frac{27}{32}$	$8\frac{3}{4}$	$7\frac{7}{8}$	$7\frac{5}{32}$	$6\frac{9}{16}$

The most widely used supplementary lenses are +1, +2, and +3 dioptres, with focal lengths of 1 m, $\frac{1}{2}$ m, and $\frac{1}{3}$ m respectively. Most manufacturers call these No 1, No 2 and No 3, but it is important to note that some Japanese manufacturers use a slightly different notation.

If you use supplementaries over a focusing lens, you can make use of the focusing adjustment to focus upon intermediate distances. Information is given in the following Tables.

USING SUPPLEMENTARY LENSES

Camera focus setting (ft)	Distance from supplementary lens to subject (in)		
	Lens No 1	Lens No 2	Lens No 3
Infinity	$39\frac{3}{8}$	$19\frac{3}{4}$	$13\frac{1}{8}$
100	$38\frac{1}{8}$	$19\frac{3}{8}$	13
50	37	19	$12\frac{7}{8}$
25	$34\frac{7}{8}$	$18\frac{1}{2}$	$12\frac{1}{2}$
20	$33\frac{3}{4}$	$18\frac{1}{4}$	$12\frac{3}{8}$
15	$32\frac{3}{4}$	$17\frac{3}{4}$	$12\frac{1}{4}$
12	30	$17\frac{1}{4}$	12
10	$29\frac{3}{8}$	$16\frac{7}{8}$	$11\frac{7}{8}$
8	$27\frac{7}{8}$	$16\frac{3}{8}$	$11\frac{1}{2}$
7	$26\frac{3}{4}$	16	$11\frac{3}{8}$
6	$25\frac{3}{8}$	$15\frac{1}{2}$	$11\frac{1}{8}$
5	$23\frac{3}{4}$	$14\frac{3}{4}$	$10\frac{3}{4}$
4	$21\frac{5}{8}$	14	$10\frac{1}{4}$
3.5	$20\frac{1}{4}$	$13\frac{3}{8}$	10
3	$18\frac{3}{4}$	$12\frac{3}{4}$	$9\frac{5}{8}$

USING SUPPLEMENTARY LENSES (METRIC SCALING)

Camera focusing setting (m)	Distance from supplementary lens to subject (cm)		
	Lens No. 1 (+1D)	Lens No. 2 (+2D)	Lens No. 3 (+3D)
Infinity	100	50	33.3
30	97	49	32.6
15	94	48.4	32.3
10	91	47.5	32
5	83	45.5	31
4	80	44	30.5
3	75	43	30
2.5	71	41.6	29
2	67	40	28.3
1.5	60	37.5	27
1.2	54.5	35.3	25.5
1.0	50	33.3	25
0.9	47	32	24.2

Title sizes and camera distances

It is a very simple matter to calculate the title size at a given distance, and with a given focal length of lens. The calculation uses the principlo of equal triangles, which represent the gate width and lens focal length on one side, and title size and distance on the other side, thus:

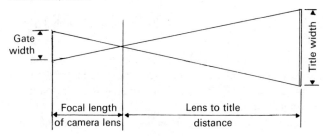

Knowing three of the dimensions on the diagram, you can readily calculate the fourth. Use this basic formula:

$$\frac{Title\ width}{Lens\text{-}to\text{-}title\ distance} = \frac{Gate\ width}{Focal\ length\ of\ camera\ lens}$$

For ease of calculation, we can transpose this into two simple formulae:

(1)   Title width $= \dfrac{Gate\ width}{Focal\ length} \times Lens\text{-}to\text{-}title\ distance$

and

(2)   Lens-to-title distance $= \dfrac{Focal\ length}{Gate\ width} \times Title\ width$

Note: For gate width, use the dimension for projector gate size, to give the size that will be seen when the film is projected. These dimensions are given below.

Example: Super 8 camera with 15 mm lens, distance (lens-to-title) 50 cm (500 mm) which is approximately $19\frac{1}{2}$ in. Gate width (see p. 29) 0.212 in or 5.36 mm. What title width will be seen on projection?

Use Formula (1):

$$Title\ width = \frac{5.36}{15} \times 500$$

$$= 172\ mm\ (approximately\ 6\tfrac{3}{4}\ in)$$

Title width refers to the actual area that will be seen when the film is projected on the screen. The title card *must* be larger than this (p. 30), to give a 'safety' margin. The lettering must be narrower than the photographed area.

When calculating title sizes, remember to use the same units throughout. That is, use either inches, or millimetres. Useful equivalents:

$$1\,mm = 0.039\,in$$
$$1\text{-metre} = 39.3\,in$$
$$1\text{-inch} = 25.4\,mm$$

TABLE OF GATE SIZES
Format width of projector aperture

Standard 8 mm	0.172 in (4.37 mm)
Super 8 or Single-8	0.212 in (5.36 mm)
16 mm	0.380 in (9.65 mm)

Photographed area

The camera you use determines what will be a convenient photo-graphed area—that is the area you will see on the screen when the film is projected. On the film you will, in fact, record slightly more than this, but the edges will be cut off by the projector gate which is slightly smaller than the camera gate.

Useful title sizes

Title sizes given in the following table have been chosen so that a non-focusing camera can be used with a readily obtainable supplementary lens, as follows:

Distance	Supplementary lens
39 in	+1 dioptre (No 1)
26 in	+1.5 dioptres
$19\frac{1}{2}$ in	+2 dioptres (No 2)
13 in	+3 dioptres (No 3)

When using a supplementary over the front of the camera lens, measure the lens-to-title distance from the supplementary.

Title sizes with supplementary lenses

Film Gauge and Lens	Distance	Title Size inches	millimetres
standard 8 mm film 13 mm lens	13 in.	$4\frac{3}{8}\times3\frac{1}{4}$	111×83
	$19\frac{1}{2}$ in.	$6\frac{1}{2}\times5$	166×125
	26 in.	$8\frac{3}{4}\times6\frac{1}{2}$	222×167
	39 in.	$13\frac{1}{8}\times9\frac{7}{8}$	333×250
Super 8 film 15 mm lens	13 in.	$4\frac{5}{8}\times3\frac{1}{2}$	118×89
	$19\frac{1}{2}$ in.	$7\times5\frac{1}{4}$	177×133
	26 in.	9.3×7	236×177
	39 in.	$13.9\times10\frac{1}{2}$	354×266
16 mm film 25 mm lens	13 in.	$4\frac{5}{8}\times3\frac{3}{4}$	128×96
	$19\frac{1}{2}$ in.	$7\frac{1}{2}\times5\frac{5}{8}$	191×143
	26 in.	$10\times7\frac{1}{2}$	255×191
	39 in.	15×11.3	382×287

Suppose you have decided to use a title area 7 in wide, which is convenient for many users—even with a simple movie camera. The format is 4:3, so the height will be three-quarters of the width; that is, the title area will be $7\times5\frac{1}{4}$ in approximately, or 177×133 mm.

Card size

One of the unforgivable things in a title is to show the edge of the card on the screen, so always use a card much larger than the filmed area. This is especially true with a non-reflex camera.
In our example of a $7\times5\frac{1}{4}$ in title, it would be wise—and convenient—to use a card of at least 10×8 in (about 25×20 cm), so that there will be plenty of safety margin outside the area being filmed. Then any slightly inaccurate line-up will not ruin the title by showing the edge of the card.

Lettering area

It takes only a little experience to judge how much to fill your picture area with lettering. This is a matter of calculating proportions of lettering to total area, or of simply knowing what looks right. Many beginners tend to go too near the edge of the picture, which then looks overfull. Less frequently, one sees tiny lettering almost lost in the centre of the picture area.

If you have a zoom reflex camera and are working within the normal range of the zoom, you can use the zoom to vary the magnification as you study the appearance of the title in the viewfinder, before beginning to shoot film at all. This is a very useful way to study the effect of varying the size of the lettering in the frame. As a general guide, the lettering should not be more than three-quarters of the total picture width (p. 33), and two-thirds usually looks quite satisfactory. You may wish to adjust this rule somewhat, as you become completely sure of the exact area you will see on the screen when projecting the film, and it also depends on the number of words in the title.

Symmetrical or not?

Symmetrical arrangements are particularly pleasing and sometimes essential. But they do demand exactness in viewfinding. If you have any doubt about the accuracy of your viewfinder, avoid critically symmetrical titles such as a long subtitle with a border all around it. It is better by far to use a simple but satisfying unsymmetrical layout. This is particularly true with titles consisting of only a few words.

Layout

With a little experience of seeing results on the screen, you will quickly develop a sense of layout. A good tip when setting out a title on the card is to use a mask to show the exact photographed area. The card itself will, of course, be larger than this, for reasons already discussed.

One of the things you will have to note is to keep the centre of the title lettering *slightly above* the centre of the frame. In other words, have *a little more room below* the lettering, than above. This avoids the optical illusion of the lettering 'dropping out of the picture'.

Variety in titles

Every film needs a main or introductory title, and an end title. The main title tells the audience what it is about to see. It may include a credit for the maker of the film, but in general a main title should be kept simple and should contain as few words as possible. For this reason, the size of the lettering can be relatively large in relation to the picture area.

Exactly how large the letters of the main title should appear in the frame is again a matter of judging layout. If you have a zoom camera of the type that lets you adjust the photographed area easily (that is, if you are within the range of the zoom, and not on macro), you can make the same size lettering appear larger or smaller just by altering the zoom. This is useful when you have only one or two sizes of type.

Do not, however, overfill the picture area if you have only a few words. For example, *The End* filling the entire screen would look quite out of proportion. As we said, with a zoom camera you can study the title in the viewfinder; you can then adjust the zoom to 'test' any title for letter size.

Subtitles

In the days of silent films, subtitles were essential for telling the story. Today, subtitles are completely out of fashion and you should avoid them—unless of course you are trying to give the effect of a film made fifty or more years ago. Nowadays we are used to receiving our information either visually or, if additional help is required, then via the soundtrack.

There are, however, films which need linking titles, and these should maintain a constant style throughout, they should, however, normally use a smaller letter size than the main title. Remember you can achieve a different letter size by different reduction

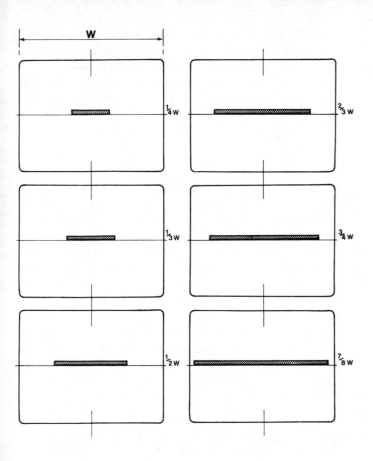

For a line of type consisting of several words, a length of $\frac{2}{3}$ picture width is best. Note that **W** is the width that appears on the screen. The photographed area is slightly larger because the camera gate is always slightly bigger than the projector gate. The title card should always be wider than the filmed area to avoid showing the edge of the card on the screen.

when filming—by adjusting the zoom setting, for example—provided you have sufficient excess area of card all around the lettering to avoid including the edge of it in your picture.

You can also use upper-case letters (capitals) for the main title, and upper and lower for the linking titles, with only the initial letter of the title and of any names to be in upper-case, and the rest in lower-case.

What to say in a title

Apart from main titles, *never* say in words what the audience can perfectly well see on the screen by watching the picture. Nor should you include what can be heard by listening to the soundtrack.

When writing the wording for titles, *keep it simple.* Do not say: 'For our holiday in 1978 we went to New York'. Imagine you are writing the proverbial telegram where words cost money! You might perfectly well say: 'New York 1978', because the audience can see perfectly well from the film that you went there on holiday. Alternatively, you could settle for: 'Holidays 1978' because the film shows that you went to New York. You might even consider using: 'Holidays 1978' superimposed on a still of the Manhattan skyline—using this simple visual instead of words to say 'New York'.

Constant letter size

When you use subtitles or linking titles in a film, assume a consistent style throughout. In particular, you should keep a *constant size of lettering.* This means that the maximum permissible letter size in the frame should be determined for the longest title. The other titles should then use the same size of letters.

If there is one title with a lot of letters in it, work out if this can be reduced somehow, and aim for approximately the same number of letters in each title. Otherwise the shorter titles may look too small in the frame.

Minimum size of lettering

Naturally you want all the words to be readable on the screen—by all your audience, no matter where they may be sitting. It is therefore necessary to specify a reasonable minimum type size. This is best done in relation to a factor of screen size and viewing distance. For example, remember that a 16 mm projector is generally provided with a 50 mm or 2 in lens, and this requires the projector to be placed approximately 5.6 screen-widths away from the screen itself. Probably not many of the audience will be sitting behind the projector, so the maximum viewing distance will be about six times the screen-width. Or, with the usual 4:3 format of width and height, this represents a maximum viewing distance of about 8 screen-heights.

Now we can relate the height of the lettering to this. As an absolute minimum for an audience with good eyesight, the letters could be as small as one-fiftieth of screen-height. Much better legibility is given if the letters are no smaller than about $\frac{1}{25}$ of screen-height, and this is a recommended figure for movie titles in the smallest lettering you will normally use. On this basis, if the filmed area of your title card is 5 in high (125 mm), the suggested minimum size lettering would be $\frac{1}{5}$ in high (5 mm).

We are talking about *minimum* type size, such as might be used on an illustration or a map or graph, or maybe a close-up extract from a book. Titles with 100 per cent wording but relatively few letters—and this accounts for most titles—will almost invariably use larger letters for this size title area: possibly $\frac{1}{2}$ in high letters, and even larger for the main title or maybe *The End.*

In the German DIN standard 19042, the recommended minimum letter size is similar whether for cine or stills, or indeed for overhead projectors. In practice it seems desirable to choose somewhat larger type when using the 8 mm gauges, for two reasons: the lower average brightness of much 8 mm and Super 8 projection, and the proportionately greater effect of slight unsteadiness in the picture.

Length of line

Movie titles must be easy to read on the screen, and one of the factors here is the number of words you can get into each line— assuming you have several lines in one title, as sometimes happens. A rather short line is desirable—considerably shorter than you will find in a book, or even in the popular newspapers. A suggested average of about *four* words per line has been found acceptable. This figure assumes average spacing. The usual 4-word line consists of approximately 22 letters and spaces. This means that for a typical typeface used for titles, the 22-word line will have a line-length of approximately 20 times the letter-height (for capital letters). One can then relate the type size to the photographed area.

Suggested type sizes for a four-word line are given in a table on page 38. This assumes the line-length is three-quarters of the photographed width or, more strictly speaking, the width that will be seen on the screen when the film is projected.

In practice, most titles will have less than the maximum number of characters quoted, so may use correspondingly larger type sizes, just as a printer will use 'display' type which is larger than most of the reading matter.

Style of type

If you look at a catalogue of printers' type, or of instant lettering which uses the same typefaces, you will see a bewildering collection. In making a choice for titling, you have to consider three factors: whether it is easily readable; whether it will photograph well; and whether the style is appropriate. To be readable, the typeface must be simple, medium to bold in 'weight' and not thin or 'wiry' or 'light'. A sans-serif face is simpler and generally preferable for photography than a Roman typeface with serifs. Do not normally choose a 'condensed' face because on the screen it looks as if the letters are crowded together which reduces readability.

Avoid fussy typefaces, and ones with curls and twirls on the letters. In particular, avoid typefaces with very thick and thin lines combined; they do not photograph well, for the thin lines tend to fill in and the heavy lines look overpowering.

If you use plastic letters for your titles you are obviously limited to the rather few typefaces available, but these are simple and usually well chosen. If you use instant lettering of the rub-down variety, you have a wide choice of faces. Even so, it is best to choose a good straightforward one. You can then use it, with

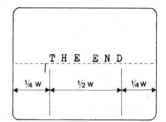

Some examples of type size, proportions and spacing to create a well-balanced title. Laying out a title on a typewriter is always a useful practice, no matter what form the final lettering is to take.

your particular layouts, to give your films your own style in titles.

Suggested basic proportions for cine titles

1 Decide the photographed area (ie: what will appear on the screen when the film is projected).
Standard cine format is 4:3 (width×height); call these W and H respectively.

2 The title card overall size should be half as large again, each way;
that is, the card size will be at least $1\frac{1}{2}W \times 1\frac{1}{2}H$, in order to allow ample room for viewfinder and line-up errors, and not include the edges of the card in-picture.

3 Line length (normal maximum line length) will be approximately three quarters of the photographed width;
that is, max line length=$\frac{3}{4}W$.
Note: this line length is also the same as H.

4 Number of letters per line.
This obviously depends on the letter height.

5 Smallest letters to be used.
Suggested minimum letter height for cine, especially the 8mm gauges, is $\frac{1}{25}$ of the photographed height—that is, $1/25 \times H$. Note, lettering can be larger, but not smaller.

6 Based on this minimum size lettering, and a line length of $\frac{3}{4}W$, a line length consists of approximately four average words.
This four-word line consists of approximately 22 characters (letters and spaces).

7 Considering the styles of lettering likely to be used for cine titles, based on a 22-character line, the height of the letters will be approximately $\frac{1}{20}$ of the line length.
Based on the standard 4:3 format shape, the height of the letters will be approximately $1/22.5 \times$ photographed height H.

8 Taking the height (H) of the photographed area, the following formulas can be used:
For a 22-character line, use letter height of $\frac{1}{22} \times H$; for a 15-character line, use letter height of $\frac{1}{15} \times H$; for a 10-character line, use letter height of $\frac{1}{10} \times H$ etc.

NOT TOO BIG

Not too small

Type size should
be in proportion
to the title

DON'T SET LETTERS
TOO TIGHTLY SPACED

Do not hyphen-
ate words in
a title

Vary type size
to achieve
EMPHASIS

Lengthy static titles
can become a bore to
read. Your audience
wants to see the film,
not to spend the time
reading unduly
long titles

Hold titles on the screen
long enough to read
the words out loud

Letter spacing . . .

too tight

too loose

Upper and lower case
lettering is much
easier to read

Choose the type size
based on the longest
title in a series

Avoid unduly
long titles . . .

A V I A T I O N

A V I A T I O N

CAPITAL LETTERS ARE FULLY
ACCEPTABLE FOR SHORT
TITLES. BUT A LONG TITLE
THAT HAS BEEN SET WHOLLY
IN CAPITALS IS ALMOST
UNREADABLE, ESPECIALLY
IF SET WITH TIGHT SPACING
OF THE LINES. WE ARE
JUST NOT USED TO READING
CAPITALS IN LARGE
QUANTITIES

T H E   E N D

Useful tips on title layout. When laying out type, remember letters should be spaced apart with optically, not mechanically, correct spacing. Narrow letters, such as I, need less width than wider letters, such as M. When letters such as A and V are together, the spacing should allow for the juxtaposed slopes of the letters.

9 In all cases, letter height is taken as being the height of a normal capital. If you are using lower-case lettering, remember this will have ascenders on letters such as b, h, k, l etc. and descenders on letters such as g, j, p, q etc.

If you have more than one line of type, space the lines sufficiently apart so that the descenders on one line do not meet the ascenders on the line below.

10 The lettering should always appear preferably just slightly above the title centre-line (in height), or possibly central, but never below centre, otherwise the letters appear to be 'dropping out of the picture'.

Title Letters and Backgrounds

Lettering and backgrounds are the stuff that titles are made of. Simple components, perhaps, yet the results can look anything from roughest amateur to smoothly professional. Everything depends on your choice of letters and your expertise and workmanship in using them. There is also a further factor—your imagination, and with it your ability to make a title which is just right for that particular film.

As soon as you add titles to a film you will see the truth of the old adage—any title is better than none at all. Even the simplest titles at the beginning and end of a film give it a charisma that lifts it above the ordinary amateur standard. Inexpensive letters, carefully used, are quite acceptable and a good way to begin your adventures into titling.

Felt and PVC sheet letters

There is a wide range of title letters from which to choose. At the lower price range of the scale are sets of punched-out felt or PVC plastic letters. Depending on the make, these can vary from the beautifully made to crudely shaped letters hardly worthy of a child's toy-set. Choose accordingly!

Sometimes these inexpensive letters are big, in which case set them into a correspondingly large photographed area. This could be an advantage if it allows you to use the camera without any additional close-focusing arrangements—depending on the camera.

Colour of lettering

The most useful colour for any title is undoubtedly *white*. White letters can be set onto either a black or a coloured background, or indeed onto a picture background of suitable size.

Many letters are also available in colours, though you will usually find these much less appropriate than white. In general, you will do well to steer clear of coloured letters at first, unless of course you have a particular reason for using them.

Black letters, too, are inappropriate for most cine titles. The reason is that if black letters are used on a white or very light background, the impression on projection will be mainly one of flicker. The use of white letters on a darkish background avoids this. However, black letters have their uses, as when superimposed on the lighter sky area of a picture background.

When selecting the colour of letters remember the old rule of white against black, or at least white against dark, for best readability.

Coloured backgrounds

One of the joys of using cut-out or moulded plastic letters is that it is so easy to lay them on attractive coloured backgrounds— but suitable ones, please! In fact, you will soon find yourself collecting all sorts of coloured cloths and papers, for use as exciting title backgrounds. Always remember that the colour of the background should be appropriate to the film, and that generally the same background colour will be used throughout one film, so ensuring consistency of style. The darker and quieter colours are the most useful because they go so well with the white lettering normally used.

Using plastic and similar letters

It is useful to start titling with plastic or similar loose letters, because they can be pushed about on the title card until the spacing and layout look just right. Most newcomers find it convenient to be able to move the lettering around after it has been set out. This makes it simple to study the effect of different spacing, and particularly to centre-up one line against another.

One of the problems in setting out lettering is to keep the lines horizontal; very few people can achieve this just by eye. It is best to work with a T-square on a drawing board, or even a straight-edged table. You can temporarily fix your title card to the drawing board with adhesive tape across the corners of the card. It is best to use the type of adhesive tape known as 'drafting tape' which peels off easily and cleanly.

By their nature, movable letters are indeed *movable* and must not be jerked after being set in place. In fact, some of the makes of letters on the market are so liable to move accidentally, that it is best to set them out on the card already taped *in situ* under the camera. Most types of loose letters are best photographed with the camera pointing directly down on to the title. A horizontal titler is not usable with some types of loose letters.

Other types of letters avoid such problems by having some degree of 'stick' when used with certain types of background material. For example, letters stamped out from plastic sheet will usually adhere fairly well to a background sheet of PVC or similar plastic. This sheet can be transparent so that it may be laid over whatever background material you wish. The adhesion is sometimes so good that you can even lift the title carefully to the vertical for filming. The letters peel off easily afterwards.

Inexpensive felt letters have the advantage of being naturally matt and thus free from surface reflection. They also cling fairly well to a felt or similar background. These felt letters are best handled with tweezers when placing them into position and lifting them off again.

Plastic moulded letters generally look much better than stamped-out letters. Moreover, moulded letters have what may be an advantage, of 'depth' that is invaluable in giving relief effects with suitably slanting lighting (p. 111). Some types of moulded letters have a faintly recessed back surface that can be pressed hard on to a slightly flexible vinyl sheet and will adhere by suction as well as the natural static attraction of the two plastic materials. In this case, the set-out title can be lifted to the vertical position for filming—though you must not be too rough with it or some of the letters may drop off.

Generally you will find it better to leave the title horizontal for filming. If you set out the lettering under the camera, note that the camera *must* be the same way up as the title. Otherwise you end up with the title appearing upside down on the screen! Materials other than plastics are sometimes used for loose letters. China clay, for example, is an excellent white matt material for letters that photograph well. But it is somewhat fragile, and you have to be careful not to squeeze the letters or they break in half.

Self-adhesive letters

Some makes of letters, both plastic and china clay, have adhesive on the back that remains tacky more or less permanently. Thus it sticks positively to a smooth surface.

But note three points: One, if you use these sticky-back letters on a paper-surfaced background, you will probably tear away the surface of the background when you remove the letters. Moreover, the paper fragments sticking to the back of the letters ruins their adhesive properties. To avoid this, stick the letters on to a sheet of transparent 'cel' or vinyl which can be laid over the background itself.

Two, while self-adhesive letters have the advantage of being usable on a vertical title without falling off, this is to some degree outweighed by the fact that each letter sticks as soon as it is laid in place on the background, and cannot be altered afterwards. You often need to adjust the position of the letters and their exact spacing. The sticky-back letters do not permit this, especially when new.

Three, the adhesive seems to deteriorate and harden with age, and eventually becomes quite ineffective. The letters can still be used, of course, but only by laying them on a flat horizontal surface — unless you buy a tube of special adhesive to recoat the back of each letter.

Magnetic letters

A particularly efficient self-adhesive lettering is the magnetic type, which is made either of die-cast metal or moulded plastic, in either case with a small magnet fixed to the back within the confines of the letter so that it does not show from the front. Sometimes a tiny bar magnet is used, while some makes use a small

ABCDefgh123

ABCDEF1234

ABCDefgh123

Professional

CINE

TITLES

One of the advantages of dry transfer letters, such as Letraset, is the wide range of typeface styles available. Plastic moulded letters obviously have a much more restricted, though useful, image.

strip of the so-called magnetic rubber, ie: a rubber strip made with a large proportion of magnetic particles in it, and then magnetized. Magnetic lettering is laid out upon a steel-backed background. It is sufficient if the background is of paper or thin card, backed with a steel sheet, since the magnetic letters will cling through the paper or thin card.

Available moulded plastic letters

There are some really excellent moulded plastic letters on the market, and quite a range from which to chose. One of the oldest established and best known is the *Presgrip* (British), with three sizes: $\frac{3}{8}$in, $\frac{9}{16}$in, and $\frac{3}{4}$in (approximately 9.5mm, 14mm and 19mm respectively). The most popular size is the $\frac{9}{16}$in, with the smaller size coming a close second, while the largest is used mostly for short titles such as *The End.*
Having several type sizes allows you to do more interesting layouts, because you can use larger letters for important words such as the title of the film, and smaller letters for the subsidiary wording.
Presgrip offers lower-case and numerals as well as the upper case; its plain *Gills Sans* type style is the most widely used as the simple design always looks right and photographs well. Roman (with serifs) and Script faces are also made.
Plastic letters are usually sold in sets. Typical *Presgrip* sets offer around 300 capitals and numerals including 15 of the letter E, or a set with upper and lower case and numerals with nearly 400 characters has 7 capital Es and 14 lower case. Larger and smaller sets are also available. Each set comes complete in a compartmented tray; an important practical feature that most users find essential for speeding up their work.

Comprehensive sets

One thing must be said about sets of letters: have plenty of them. Once you have decided on a particular style and make of lettering, buy as large a set as you reasonably can. This is especially important if you plan to do titles with more than a few words. Even a four-line sub-title or credit title will use about 80 letters, and for setting this without running short of some characters, you will almost certainly need a set containing at least 15 of the letter E, for example. Subtitles generally look best set in lower case, except of course for the start of a sentence, a place name or the name of a person, which usually will each be a capital letter. So do have plenty of letters. Nothing is more frustrating than to run out of certain letters just before the title wording is complete.

Magnetic and sticky-back letters

One of the happy features about both magnetic and sticky-back letters is that they can be supplied stuck to a plastic-surfaced carrier (with steel insert, for the magnetic letters, of course) which is attractive proposition from the marketing point of view. It also permits the letters to be displayed—in a shop window, for example—without dropping off. Some of these sets are rather small—typically around 120 letters in a set—and if you plan to make longer wordings you may find you have to buy two sets. A typical manufacturer of magnetic letters is Hama in West Germany, with a set of 120 letters 20 mm high (approximately $\frac{3}{4}$ in) with a depth (they call it height) of 4 mm which is useful for relief lighting (p. 000). Another Hama magnetic letter set uses the serif *Antiqua* typeface and gives 120 letters 14 mm (approximately $\frac{9}{16}$ in) high, and a depth of 2 mm. These sets are made in white, which is the most useful, with alternative colours of red, yellow and blue.

Another maker of magnetic letters in West Germany is Rowi, with a set of 120 letters in the plain and suitable Helvetica typeface; here again the letters are 20 mm high and 4 mm deep, with five of the letter E in the set. All these sets are capitals and numerals. In self-adhesive plastic letters, there is quite a range, and one of the best-known makes is Hernard (USA), with letters made of white matt china clay. Sizes of available letters include $\frac{3}{8}$ in, $\frac{3}{4}$ in, and $1\frac{1}{4}$ in high, and sets have from 110 letters upwards in several different styles. The *Medium Gothic* typeface is perhaps the most useful.

West Germany too, has taken to supplying plastic moulded sticky-back types in attractively presented sets and, for example, Rowi have sets of 140 capitals and numerals 10 mm high (and 1.8 mm deep) with 11 of the letter E per set. Another set has letters 15 mm high, and yet another letters 20 mm high, with a depth of 4 mm, again useful for relief effects with slanting lighting.

Hama offer sets of sticky-back letters, with two styles of type, capitals and numerals. One style supplies letters 14 mm high (2 mm deep) with 128 characters in a set, while the other set has 100 characters 20 mm high (4 mm deep). Each of these sets is available in white—the most useful—as well as various colours. Tubes of adhesive are also listed for renewing the back surface.

The Presgrip letters (Britain) are also available in sticky-back form, in sets of 178 characters, $\frac{9}{16}$ in high (approximately 14 mm), with a tube of adhesive included in each set.

Letters moulded in 'trees'

One of the interesting facets of plastic-moulding techniques is that a multi-unit job can be moulded in one piece on what is known as a 'tree'. The Cervin letters, for example, made in France, are produced in this way and sold as a complete 'tree' from which the individual letters may be carefully cut with sharp scissors. You can buy several of these 'trees' of letters to make up a larger set.

One of the problems with small plastic-moulded letters is that they are very light in weight, so you have to be careful not to disturb them after laying out before filming. Letters of this sort can only be used with the title card lying horizontally.

Setting out

Whatever kind of individual letters you use, you have to set them out on your chosen title card or background with a good-looking layout, and in straight lines with proper spacing.

Perhaps the most difficult thing is to set the letters down in straight lines. A useful tip here is to lay them along a ruler or, better, a T-square, with the bottom of each letter lying along the straight edge.

It is helpful to have one of the systems where the letters are set out, not on the background itself, but on a transparent cel or vinyl sheet. A system of this nature is used by *Presgrip*. The transparent sheet can then be laid over a ruled-out guide sheet which saves much time and labour.

Presgrip supply a special ruler for laying out the letters which has 0 in the centre and measures equally on either side. This is useful when setting out symmetrical titles accurately around the centre-line.

Instant transfer letters

Perhaps the greatest invention of all time for amateur title makers is the instant transfer type lettering, of which *Letraset* is the best known example. These letters are available in a huge range of type styles and sizes. They tend to be expensive when you have a lot of titles to do. But they add a professionalism and polish to your titles provided, of course, you take reasonable care in setting out the letters.

Letraset and similar systems are available with white or black letters—the latter selling mostly to commercial artists and sometimes essential for superimposed titles, for example, on some light-toned pictures, as well as for a certain type of rather stylish title on a textured lighter-toned background. Coloured lettering is also made in some typefaces, for those who want special effects. This is sometimes used for making the original master films, gener-ally reversal originals, for superimposed titles made by double-printing.

The earliest *Letraset* was a wet-transfer process, and one of their first products to be marketed was a cine titling outfit. This was quickly superseded by their current dry-transfer process which consists of relatively thick ink letters printed on to a wax-surfaced translucent sheet. Each sheet of letters is protected by a sheet of 'release' paper against the letters, which will not transfer accident-ally to its surface.

For use, you take the sheet of letters, and lay it letter side down on to your title card. Now you carefully position the next letter that you want to transfer. When in exactly the correct position you rub the back of the letter through the backing sheet with a stylus or an empty ball-pen. This presses it on to the title card or background.

The adhesion here is greater than that of the letter to its waxed carry-sheet, so the letter transfers to the title card.

Obviously you need a lot of care, if not actual skill, to achieve a good line-up and correct letter-spacing. To help with both of these, most sheets of transfer letters now have small guide-line markers under each individual letter (*Letraset Spacematic* system). Each successive letter is aligned by registering its marker with the one from the previous letter. After all have been transferred, the tiny markers can be removed with adhesive tape.

This is a neat and invaluable system for achieving a professional artist's standard of line-up. A light pencil guide-line can, of course, be drawn horizontally across the title card to help keep the marks, and hence the letters, perfectly straight.

Without any such system of letter alignment you naturally have to judge the correct letter spacing. For example, you have to allow for the fact that sloping letters such as A and V need their spacing to be adjusted so that their 'slopes' lie together and do not look unduly far apart. You even have to make some allowance for this when using the guide-dash system.

The secret of using dry-transfer lettering is to take it easy; do not try to rush the job. Work with the precision of a draughtsman and, if possible, use the same tools: T-square and square on a drawing board to which you can tape the title card to hold it in position as you work.

It is often helpful to draw the title in layout form, full-size, on a spare sheet of paper. This is especially important for symmetrical layouts correctly centred on the centre-line of the photographed title area.

The accurate full-size guide is all the more important if you are doing multi-line subtitles with the lines of type 'justified' at both ends—that is, with each line starting and ending at exactly the same position across the width as the other lines. Justification, as it is called, is only really needed where several lines of type are used, and it is always harder to set out the letters in this style. The beginner should avoid it.

Carefully made title cards using Letraset or similar dry-transfer lettering can look completely professional, even when filmed with a simple amateur camera.

ABCDEFGHIJKLMNOPQRSTUVWXYZ $\frac{1}{100}$

ABCDEFGHIJKLMNOPQRSTUVWXYZ $\frac{1}{50}$

ABCDEFGHIJKLMNOPQRSTUVWXYZ $\frac{1}{40}$

ABCDEFGHIJKLMNOPQRSTUVWXYZ $\frac{1}{30}$

ABCDEFGHIJKLMNOPQRSTU $\frac{1}{20}$

ABCDEFGHIJKLMN $\frac{1}{10}$

GOOD EXAMPLE
bad example

Size of lettering in the frame, seen as a proportion of screen height. Note that anything smaller than 1/30 screen height is unreadable to the average viewer. The choice of typeface is also important for legibility, the illustration shows a good and bad example of typeface in this respect.

Typewritten titles

From the earliest days of amateur movies, typewritten titles have been a popular method of making titles with quite tidy lettering very quickly and easily.

Early in the history of 16 mm movies, long before 8 mm was even thought about, Kodak made a 'Typewriter Titler' for their 16 mm Cine-Kodak camera of that era. The camera was automatically lined up with the title frame when it was screwed to the titler. A supplementary lens of the correct power was fixed just in front of the camera lens as part of the titler and brought the image into focus at the short camera-to-title distance. Accurate locating points for the camera allowed it to be put back into the same position every time.

To use typewritten titles you must obviously have a camera that will let you film relatively small title cards. Also, it is more useful if you can cover not just one size of title card but a range of sizes; in this way you can alter the apparent size of the lettering by changing the magnification or, more properly, the degree of reduction. So if you have only one or two words in a title—*The End* for example—you can make them appear larger than if you have a multi-word title. For remember, with a typewriter, all your lettering will obviously be the same size.

The ordinary typewriter generally has one or other of two basic type sizes: *Pica* with 10 letters per linear inch along the line, and *Elite* which has 12 letters per inch. For titles, Pica is generally the more useful because it is slightly larger. So apart from giving not quite such tiny title cards, any imperfections in the letters tend to be a little less significant.

Best of all for titles are typewriters with carbon ribbon, special typeface, and proportional spacing; the IBM Executive is one well known example. Proportional spacing means that a narrow letter such as an I will occupy less space than a wide letter like an M.

Making photographic title cards

If you have facilities for doing your own photography, you can extend the scope of title-making in several different directions.

Here are some ways of using photography for making title cards:

1 Suppose you wish to make typewritten titles but want them to be white letters on a black background. This is simple. Type your title on tracing paper or matt film as used in drawing offices, and then use this as a 'negative' from which you make a contact print—or even an enlargement—in the darkroom. To obtain a good impression on the typewriter you can either use one with a carbon ribbon, or alternatively you can put a sheet of tracing paper between two sheets of new carbon paper, and use the typewriter in the 'cut stencil' mode. This gives a perfect impression on both the back and front of the tracing paper and good opacity. Having typed the wording, you use this as the original for printing, ending up by developing, fixing and washing the print in the normal way. This is particularly useful for making titles to suit cameras that take small title cards (for example the Elmo 103T and 104T), especially if you want white letters on a black background so that you can superimpose the lettering on the subject in front of the main lens of the camera.

2 You can use loose letters—such as plastic moulded letters—to make title cards on bromide paper by 'contact printing' the letters on to sensitive paper under the enlarger. Lay the letters on the bromide paper in the darkroom, with the bromide paper held normally in a masking frame under the enlarger, and without any negative in the carrier, of course. The letters are laid out carefully with a ruler for good alignment, using the normal bromide safe-lighting. The enlarger acts purely as a light source for exposing the paper evenly all over, to a good black, except where protected by the letters which, of course, hold back the light and therefore print white. You thus make excellent title 'cards' with white letters on a black background.

3 The whole business of making title cards, even on an amateur basis, is rather akin to work in a graphics studio. Similarly, one can always make very good use of a graphic arts or copy camera, in ways the professional graphics man sometimes takes for granted. For example, you can do a paste-up job of lettering, which will look somewhat rough because of all the edges of the strips of paper carrying the letters. Photograph it, using high contrast copy film, generally called *line film* or *reproduction film*. The negative will still show the edges of the pasted-up strips which come out as white lines on the jet black background of the negative. These unwanted lines are then painted out with photo-opaque compound. Alternatively the lines can be covered over with strips of deep red adhesive tape made especially for this sort of work.

Line negatives made on the process camera or copy camera are generally fairly large, often same-size with the finished job, so that they can be contact-printed on to bromide paper. Alternatively, of course, the negatives can be made smaller (or even larger) and then finally enlarged (or reduced) to the final size desired. Contact printing is readily done by using a printing frame, or even a specially made printing box.

On a rather less professional scale—since relatively few people have access to a process camera—it is perfectly practical to photograph the 'copy' on, say, a 4×5 in camera, using sheets of line film and to enlarge after retouching to give the final copy size that is required. Naturally you must have your camera set up square-on and centred on the copyboard—which can quite well be the wall—with the original artwork pinned on or temporarily stuck on with adhesive tape of the *drafting tape* variety that removes easily afterwards. The copy must be evenly lit and the usual arrangement is to have two lamps each at 45 deg. to the centre of the copyboard.

Even the owner of a 35 mm SLR camera can easily make copy negatives of line originals by using one of the microfilm negative materials. These films have superbly high resolution and give excellent contrast, though you should not aim for a completely dense maximum black. Best results on microfilm today can be obtained by working to a darkish grey rather than a full black, as the maximum density.

A supply problem with 35 mm microfilm is that it can only be ordered in bulk lengths, so you have to load your own cassettes—in the dark, of course, since the film is panchromatic. Note that you should order it *perforated,* because a lot of microfilm is supplied unperforated for use in special cameras. Some suppliers have rather large minimum order requirements, but you can generally find a sympathetic dealer who can supply the film in tins of approximately 100 ft (30 m).

Even without microfilm it is still possible to make perfectly printable line negatives by using slow pan type negative material such as Panatomic X or Pan F. The negatives can be enlarged on to contrasty bromide paper.

Generally, glossy paper will be used, either glazed or unglazed, though one of the smooth and grainless *pearl* surfaces is also suitable. The important thing is not to use a grained or semi-matt paper with a surface that will pick up light and give a speckled effect.

Once you have facilities for making good line copy negatives and prints, including opaquing out any unwanted lines etc, you will be able to employ some interesting lettering techniques much favoured by professional graphics studios.

4   You can put your lettering work out to a professional photo-lettering service, obtaining from them the words you want to use ready 'set', having been photo-printed on to strips of sensitive paper, and then developed. These companies use special machines that print one letter at a time with correct spacing and accurate alignment. This photo-lettering is generally supplied in strips about 50 mm (2 in) wide. Various typefaces are available, depending on the master letter-discs that the company has in stock. Most of these machines permit a range of enlargement so that you can order whatever size of lettering you need, in upper and lower case, as you wish.

The photo-lettering companies exist mainly to supply the needs of those doing artwork for litho platemaking which happen to be very similar to those of cine title making. The strips of photo-lettering are normally supplied with black letters on a white background. In this case, if you want white-on-black, you have to include a photographic reversal stage. You can either print your negative on to film (not paper), to make a 'positive' from which you can then make the bromide prints or, if you have suitable materials, you can do actual reversal processing (*see* Appendix). Depending on your camera and darkroom equipment, you can contact-print your negative on to line film, or perhaps even pro-jection print it by using the enlarger, and in the latter case you can change the size if required.

Strips of photo-lettering are cut into the lines of words ready to be laid out on the title cards. Then comes the paste-up stage: you stick the lines of lettering on to cards of the required overall size. Most professionals use rubber-gum for this operation. It has the advantage that you can peel it off again, using a few drops of lighter fuel, if necessary, to soften the original rubber solution.

The completed card is photographed on to the high-contrast film. The finished negative is then placed over a light-box for retouching with photo-opaque compound, and all the unwanted lines filled in, together with any pinholes and other blemishes. Finally the negative is printed to make the final title card.

5   One of the advantages of being able to retouch the negative is that you can take out any guide-lines on the artwork,

6   By making the final print on line-film (not paper), you can make an overlay film, usually with black lettering on clean film, so that the lettering can be laid over either a picture background, or some special background material. You can also use an overlay of this type for the separated-background filming of a title (*see* p. 5, colour plates).

7   It is sometimes convenient to film lettering against a light-box, and here again film overlays are most useful. Generally the film will have clear lettering on a black background. The photo-opaque will not show at all, since it will be lit from behind. Red tape opaquing should not be used for this work but opaque back tape is suitable.

Filming Your Title

The zoom reflex camera is the best thing that ever happened for titling. It has revolutionized title making, not because of the zoom, but because of the reflex viewfinder. With a reflex you view your title through the taking lens itself, and you see the viewfinder image sharp, in a sharp-edged frame.

This is obviously of inestimable value when lining up the camera and title. In fact, it enables you to shoot titles quite freely, without being tied to any fixed set-up of camera holder and title card. Yet it gives you the assurance of having seen your exact line-up in the viewfinder before you start shooting.

Compared to this, titling with a non-reflex camera is almost like shooting 'blind', but it can be done and indeed, is being done, on the basis of a more or less fixed and tested set-up. Sometimes this is most easily arranged by using a titler (*see* p. 79) which includes means for attaching the camera in exact alignment every time.

With a reflex camera, the viewfinder lets you see almost exactly what you shoot; *almost* exactly because in fact you generally need to check your viewfinder accuracy (*see* p. 62) and thereafter allow for any minor errors. This is something you need do once and for all, with a particular camera, and you are strongly advised to make this check, particularly if you will be shooting titles that really need great accuracy—symmetrical layout titles, for example, or titles surrounded by a border.

Apart from making this viewfinder test and allowing for any inaccuracies in your camera, the whole business of shooting titles with a reflex camera is supremely easy. You line up visually, focus and shoot.

The camera support

If you do many titles you may think it worthwhile to have a title stand to hold the camera, title and, if need be, the lights as well.

Some moviemakers use a ready-made titler, others make their own (*see* p. 104). One thing is sure: you should *never* try to hand-hold your camera when shooting a title. Titles must always look rock-steady on the screen, and this can only be achieved if the camera is on a really firm support. At the simplest level, you can make perfectly good and highly professional titles with the camera on a tripod and the title card pinned or taped to the wall. Use proper photo-lamps, or daylight, as appropriate.

Horizontal or vertical

One of the fundamental decisions to make about your set-up is whether to shoot your titles with the camera pointing horizontally or vertically.

With loose title letters it is much better to point the camera vertically downwards, with the title on the floor or on a fairly low support (*see* p. 61). With this arrangement you need a tripod (or other support for the camera) which is really firm. Remember that because the camera is pointing vertically downwards it will slightly overhang from the tripod top. The degree of overhang will be more extreme when the camera has a long handgrip underneath its body, and the tripod socket in the base of the grip.

Some tripods do not allow you to tilt the head as far down as 90 degrees so obviously are not suitable for this set-up. Some cameras on other tripod tops do not let you tilt through 90 degrees because the camera may foul part of the tripod. This is especially true on cameras with the tripod socket in the body behind a non-collapsible grip. The protruding grip then prevents the camera being swung to the 90 degree downwards position, because the grip fouls the top of the tripod.

To some extent, then, you must choose your tripod according to the basic design of your camera. Remember that your title card lies between two of the legs of the tripod. You must of course, aim the camera centrally between two of the tripod legs. Obviously the lights have to be placed so that the tripod legs do not cast shadows across the title, which is usually simple to arrange.

The neatness and general practicality of a vertical set-up depends a lot on your optics. If you have a zoom lens that will not focus

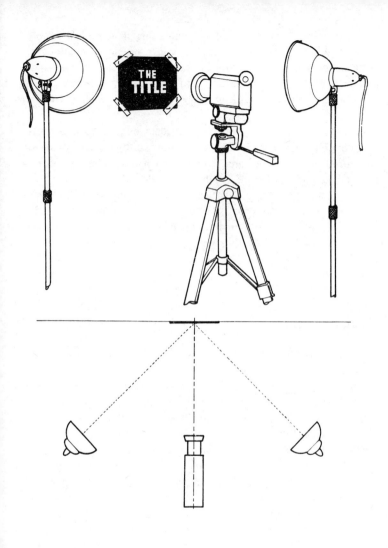

Simple horizontal set-up for shooting titles with a reflex movie camera. Pin the title card to the wall and light with two lamps at 45 degrees to the title, sufficiently far away to ensure even illumination. Set the camera on a firm tripod, centred on the title and at a distance to take in the desired area of title.

closer than 5 ft (1.5 m), and you are using it without a supplementary lens, you clearly have a rather unwieldy arrangement for which you would need a tripod certainly higher than average. If your camera will focus down to 4 ft (1.2 m) or, better still, to around 3 ft or 3.3 ft (1 m), you have a highly convenient working set-up.

In each of these cases you can set the distance (title-to-film-plane) accurately with a measuring tape, then set this distance on the focusing scale of the lens. This is almost always more accurate than visual focusing through the viewfinder.

Never forget: your title must always be *the same way up* as your camera. That is, the base of your title must correspond with the base of your camera. Your title will of course be seen the correct way up in the viewfinder, when you look into the viewfinder the normal way round—camera base towards you, in a vertical set-up.

Reflex viewfinders

The easy way to shoot titles is to use a camera with a through-the-lens reflex viewfinder. Were it not that there are so many perfectly good non-reflex cameras in use, particularly on 16 mm where the cost of the latest equipment tends to restrict its use, it is undoubtedly best to say *if you want to shoot titles, get a reflex camera.* For the users of non-reflex models, methods of lining up the camera and title are discussed fully at the end of this section (*see* p. 68). A reflex viewfinder lets you *see* what you will be filming. You look through the taking lens itself so there is no parallax. You can use the zoom to include more or less of your title without having to move the camera to and fro. It is all very convenient and easy.

How accurate is a reflex?

In the reflex viewfinder you are looking at a frame which is not the film-gate itself, but a completely separate frame set which matches the camera gate as closely as possible.

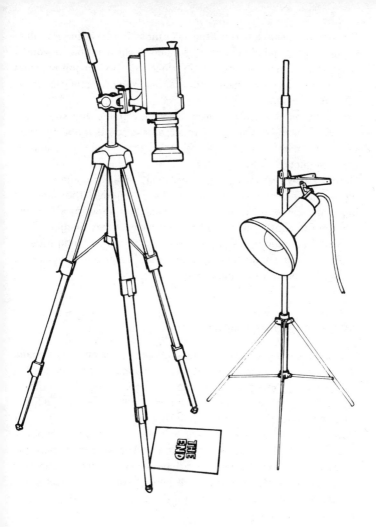

Simple vertical set-up for shooting titles with a reflex camera. Camera-to-title distance is arranged so that the required title width is included. Use one or more lamps, angled downwards to give even illumination of the title area. This set-up is particularly suitable when using loose letters which can be manipulated on the title card. The base of the camera and base of the title card must be the same way round.

On the very best cameras, especially those aimed at more profes-sional users, a genuine attempt is made to show in the viewfinder what you will see on the screen when you project the resultant film and when you use a correctly standardized projector gate of the same high accuracy.

Especially on the 8mm gauges where the frame you see in the viewfinder is only about $\frac{1}{4}$ in (6 mm) or less across, correct setting of this to match the camera gate is no mean feat. Few cameras reach perfection in this respect.

Unfortunately, when making titles, many amateur cameras show more on the film than you see in the viewfinder. Thousands of big-name cameras are made every year that show maybe 5 per cent, or more, extra all around as a so-called safety margin.

Provided you know this you can allow for it when lining up your titles. So you should certainly test your camera for viewfinder accuracy. This is very simple to do.

How to check your viewfinder

Set up a plain title card, blank sheet of paper, or even a blackboard, and line up the camera in front of it at a suitable distance so that the viewfinder image is well inside the edges of the card or black-board. Have the camera on a firm tripod or other support, and focus it on the plane of your card or blackboard.

Now you must ask an assistant to help you for a few minutes. Look through the viewfinder and ask your assistant to mark the exact position on the blackboard or paper of each of the four edges of the frame. You must tell him where to mark each edge as you look into the finder. Then draw a bold X precisely through each of the four points.

If you are a lone worker and cannot find anyone to help you, you can draw the correctly proportioned frame (4:3 proportions exactly) with the X drawn through each edge.

Now film your drawn frame with it lined up *exactly* with the edges of your viewfinder. The X on each line helps you align it with the edge of the frame in the viewfinder. Your test target does not have to be any particular size as long as you adjust the camera distance and the zoom, so that the four X marks come on the respective four edges of the frame. For example, your drawn frame can be 20×15 in or 500×375 mm, and you can pin this chart to the wall, set up your camera on a tripod opposite the chart at a suitable distance, focus, and film the test chart with the drawn edges exactly fitting your viewfinder frame.

With a zoom lens you obviously have a choice of distances and focal lengths. It will be easiest to choose a medium-to-long setting of the zoom and set the camera distance accordingly. Then you can use the zoom for final adjustment of the drawn frame to fit exactly with the edges of your viewfinder frame. Having ensured exact alignment of the reference X marks on all four edges of the finder, shoot a few seconds of film on it.

When the film is returned from processing, project it in the normal way and see how well the four Xs correspond with the edges of your projector aperture. First note the side-to-side accuracy. Evaluation of this is quite straightforward.

You may be quite suprised at the considerably less than perfect accuracy your camera shows. If you cannot believe the results you can always repeat the test!

Vertical accuracy

The top-to-bottom accuracy must also be studied with reference to *framing* of the picture, with the framing adjustment on the projector. Of course, many cameras are not as accurate as one might wish with regard to the setting of the frame-line position, which is why you may have found that film from different cameras may require re-framing on the projector. On cameras, framing is not normally adjustable, so if you use only one camera adjust your title line-up to that.

When evaluating your viewfinder accuracy from top-to-bottom you are advised to move the framing of the projector appreciably up and down, to see if your X marks at top and bottom are approximately equally spaced relative to the frame-line. In other words, the distance from the top X to the frame-line above it, should be approximately the same as the distance between the bottom X and the lower frame-line.

Is your projector gate accurate?

Needless to say, the accuracy of your projector gate can affect the accuracy of your evaluation. But most of the better manufacturers nowadays achieve relatively high accuracy in setting their gates in manufacture. The important dimension sideways is the distance between the gate aperture and the guided edge of the film—that is, the fixed edge-guides on the projector. This can be, and usually is, set with good accuracy on the factory jigs. The other edge of the film has sprung edge-guides and these hold the film against the fixed guides. This ensures that any width variations in the film will be taken up, and any tendency to weave sideways is properly controlled.

True, some projectors are encountered even today with sadly inaccurate gates, and because of the likelihood of at least some variation being found between different projectors, you are advised to avoid exactly symmetrical titles. In particular, avoid titles with a frame around the wording, since these will look most un-professional if projected on a machine which makes them look lopsided.

Exposure

At one time, giving the correct exposure was the major problem in all moviemaking, but not now. Almost all modern cameras have built-in fully-automatic metering: point the camera and the lens aperture sets itself.

Even with these fully-automatic models, however, there are a few points to watch, which is why many cameras include full manual override of the metering system. You can then set the lens aperture to any desired stop—usually after you have used the internal automatic metering system as a reference.

All the automatic metering cameras work on the same principle: they 'look at' the subject and 'read' how much light is reflected from it and into the lens on the camera. Inherently therefore, automatic metering cameras are calibrated (set-up in manufacture) on the notion of an assumed 'average subject' that reflects a

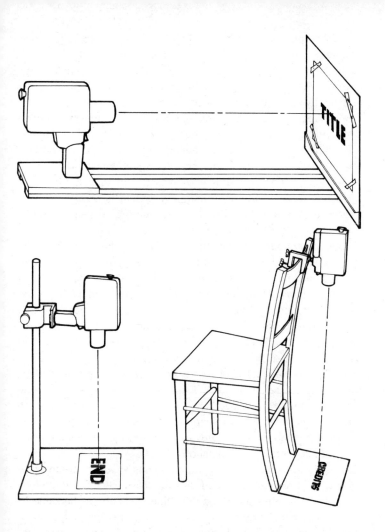

Top Simple horizontal titler, using two wooden slats as the bed. The platform must be made to suit the camera used, so that the lens is at the same height as the centre of the title. **Bottom left** Vertical set-up, using the column and clamp of a conventional enlarger. The base of the camera must be the same way round as the base of the title. **Bottom right:** With a camera clamp-type mounting, a chair back makes an excellent titler but the distance is not adjustable and title size and camera focusing must suit the height of the chair.

known proportion of the light. This 'average subject' is generally assumed to be of about 18 per cent reflectivity overall.

As long as you shoot subjects with around this average reflectivity, you will have well exposed films. Happily, most subjects are sufficiently 'average' not to need any special treatment.

The exception in ordinary filming is a very dark subject against a disproportionately light background, and you can allow for this by setting the lens aperture manually. In titling, your sometimes wish to take some decidedly non-average subjects. The classic case perhaps is a few words in white lettering against a jet black background. Any automatic metering system is bound to over-expose this. The metering system will see the subject as unduly dark, and will open up the lens aperture accordingly.

If your camera has automatic metering and a full manual override, that is, allowing you to set the lens aperture manually, you can best handle these non-average subjects by using the *grey card* method. Kodak supply sheets of special grey card with 18 per cent reflectance, and you can place one of these over your title while you read the lens aperture using the camera's own internal metering system. If you are taking a large title, you may need to use two sheets of the grey card taped together.

Read the light reflected from the grey card, not the indicated aperture on the camera's scale of *f* numbers. Then set this aperture manually using the override; take away the grey card and shoot the title. If your camera has a simple meter lock instead of override, just lock the reading on the grey card, take away the card and – still holding the aperture locked – shoot the title.

You may have a camera with a plus-minus exposure control that nevertheless remains automatic. In this case, set the plus-minus control so that the camera on your title reads about the same as on the grey card with the normal setting of the metering system; this will probably be one or two stops smaller (ie: *minus* exposure) when filming a white-on-black title. Such a title is, however, one of the very few subjects you encounter that needs a minus setting.

Even so, the current trend is not to use a jet-black background, but instead to use a moderately dark colour, and in most such cases you can achieve good results simply by shooting with the metering

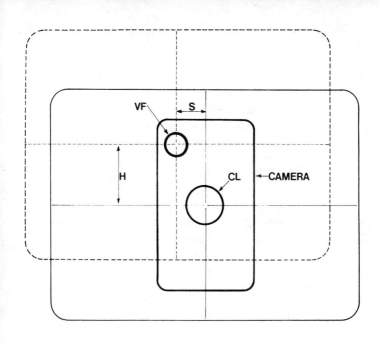

Using a non-reflex viewfinder: because the viewfinder (**VF**) is on a different centre-line from the camera lens (**CL**), the nominal field of view seen through the viewfinder (dotted) is displaced from the view being taken by the camera lens (full line). The displacement is by the same amount as the viewfinder is displaced sideways (**S**) and in height (**H**) from the axis of the camera lens.

system on normal. The automatic metering system copes incredibly well with almost all title subjects since they are all reasonably 'average' in tonal level.

Lining up a non-reflex

If you have a non-reflex camera, you do not have the opportunity to look through the viewfinder and see what you will be filming. Instead, you have to use a combination of methods to align the camera with the title.

1 Using the viewfinder and allowing for parallax as best you can; on many cameras this will be found surprisingly, often hopelessly, inaccurate. With the simple reversed Galilean viewfinders, for example, you do not see the edges of the frame as sharp, and this gives great ambiguity. For this reason most viewfinders of this design appear to include far less of the subject than will actually be recorded on the film.

2 Calculating the title size at a given distance, or alternatively the distance for a given title size (*see* p. 30). This generally works out to be surprisingly accurate.

3 Using an alignment gauge in conjunction with the non-reflex viewfinder as a means of allowing for parallax error. This is a good aid to centring, though by no means infallible because so much depends on how accurately you place your eye behind the spyhole of the viewfinder eyepiece.

4 Careful measurement, setting the camera-to-title distance as accurately as possible. This may be the title-to-film-plane, or if you use a supplementary lens it is generally title-to-supplementary distance. Some manufacturers have now adopted the film-plane as the reference point even with a supplementary in use. Follow the manufacturer's instructions on this point.

5 Careful setting of trueness by eye, where neccessary. If the title looks a bit askew when you sight it from behind the camera, you probably need to attend to the alignment.

Making a title line-up gauge

A title line-up gauge for a non-reflex camera has to be tailor-made for that particular camera and lens, and for the title size you will be using.

You must start by doing the calculation of title size at your given distance, with your focal length of lens. Then take a sheet of card, rather larger than your calculated title size, and draw on the card the outline of the title size. Use a moderately thick black felt-tipped pen. Draw also the diagonals from corner to corner, and clearly mark the intersection—which is the centre-point of the title area.

Now look at your camera and you can see that the viewfinder—being a non-reflex—is displaced somewhat from the axis of the taking lens. The finder may be sideways displaced, or vertically, or more usually a bit of both. Measure the distance between the camera lens and the centre of the viewfinder. Suppose for example it were to be 1 in to the side of the lens and 1 in above it. Draw a new centre point, using a red felt-tipped pen this time to differentiate it from the frame you have drawn already, the new point being (continuing our example) the same 1 in sideways and 1 in above the original centre point, in the direction as seen from the rear of the camera. Add also the similarly displaced frame, the same size as the original black frame, and draw the diagonals to emphasize the centre-point. All this frame should be in red.

Your guide card now has the two title areas and centre points. One is in black, representing the view seen by the camera lens. The other is in red representing the view from the viewfinder position. Remember that our example has mentioned 1 in displacement, but your own card will of course have the exact displacement for your particular camera, between the taking lens and the viewfinder.

Now you can set up the guide card in front of the camera at the prescribed distance, and line up the red centre point in the centre of your viewfinder. When this is correctly set, the camera lens will be properly lined up with the title area—which is the black frame—or at least with as good accuracy as your use of the viewfinder allows. Take care to keep your eye exactly central behind the spyhole. Preferably you should do this lining up for the first time when you have some film in your camera and can use a few inches of it for a test. When the film is returned from processing, you can project it and see exactly how much of your title card will be seen on the screen—and, of course, how well centred it is. You should see your black-ink frame just nicely filling the screen area, but it is doubtful if you will achieve such accuracy on your first test.

It is often helpful to draw numbered scales across each of the four edges of the black frame on your guide-card, so that you can see, on projection, the exact points on all four edges that represent your frame limits.

Having prepared your guide-card, and checked its accuracy with a film-test, you can use it at any time to line up your camera with a title (representing the black frame area) by looking into the non-reflex viewfinder and lining up on the red frame, or at least centring on the red centre-point. When setting up, remember that careful measurement is always essential for the camera to give your desired degree of reduction (ie: to take in a particular title size).

You may find it necessary to sight the line of your camera against the line of the title, to check squareness in each direction. With careful examination of your set-up, you may see and be able to eliminate some unexpected errors. Nothing looks worse than a title with lines of crooked letters. To show the words sloping downhill is unforgivable!

A line-up problem which occasionally occurs is when the base of camera is not quite square with the rest of its body. Careful sighting of the camera against the title reveals this immediately.

Optical centring methods

A useful dodge to assist centring of the camera and title is to use a piece of mirror held perfectly flat against the front of the lens. This obviously depends on the fact that virtually all lenses are very carefully made with the body of the lens and its front dead square to the lens axis. You also need a title card with a bold cross drawn at its centre, and a hole punched through the card at this exact centre point.

The idea is that now you look from *behind* the title card, *through* the central hole, and you will see the cross on the title card which is reflected in the mirror. Adjust the title position (or the camera) until the cross is seen properly central.

Such a method has been marketed by *Presgrip*, whose titler unit has an open-backed frame allowing you to look through the hole in the title-centring card.

Gate viewers

For the many owners of non-reflex cameras—particularly 16 mm—that are still perfectly serviceable, there is the obvious dodge of putting a piece of matt film, or even tracing paper, in the camera gate, opening the shutter, and looking at the image on the matt film. This, of course, requires that the camera's pressure plate can be taken out readily and that the gate is then freely accessible. Some cameras such as the later Bolex H16 models have a removable gate pressure plate unit, and this can be replaced with a prism type look-through.

On certain other cameras with removable gate unit, it is possible to make up a simple holder for a small prism or piece of mirror (preferably front-silvered) behind the gate, and this can be used in conjunction with the piece of matt film mentioned above.

Many years ago, Kodak used to make a particularly neat gate look-through unit for their 16 mm magazine-loading cameras. This unit simply fitted in place of the film-magazine and had telescope type optics and an eyepiece that gave an excellent view of the image in the gate.

Naturally when using any sort of gate look-through device, the camera must be stopped with the shutter fully open. One or two cameras provide for this, for 'time' exposures, but with other cameras you have either to run down the spring motor, or in the case of electric drive models, to disconnect one of the batteries while the camera is running, and to do this several times until the shutter happens to stop fully open. You can see this by looking into the lens from the front of the camera.

Obviously the camera must not be loaded with film when you want to use any sort of gate viewer.

Projected gate

A variation on the gate look-through idea is to shine a light back through the gate—again, with the shutter open.

At its simplest, a torch may be held behind the gate. More elaborately, a small lamp can be used, perhaps with small condenser lenses. In this case the condensers would be arranged to collect light from the lamp filament, and to condense this as a circle of light just large enough to cover the camera gate. The condenser focal length should be such that it forms an image of the lamp filament, approximately in the plane of the camera lens or just beyond it.

With well-chosen condenser lenses, you can achieve a beautifully bright image of the gate aperture, projected upon the title-card by the camera lens. Naturally the lens should be at full aperture when doing this. Even a torch bulb held behind the gate is a most useful check on line-up, and the simple arrangement will let you see picture limits, even if you have to move the lamp around slightly to achieve coverage of all four edges.

Camera gate aperture size

When using the camera gate for lining up and studying picture limits, you must remember that the projector gate is always slightly smaller than the camera gate. This is deliberate, so that your picture will always go out to the edges of your projected frame, and indeed overlap them.

The degree to which the projector gate is smaller than the camera gate varies somewhat between the gauges, there being less overlap on Super 8, for example. Remember, too, that the camera gate need not be particularly accurate as regards symmetry etc, provided it is larger than the projector gate by at least the standardized degree. Tolerances upwards are relatively wide.

You should therefore regard the camera gate aperture as only approximate when using it for the more demanding line-ups. But it is certainly good enough for initial tests, and in some cases it is invaluable.

Note incidentally that the gate aperture itself is not necessarily the exact size of the image on the film, because the gate aperture is slightly removed from the film. With a wide-angle lens, the effective size will be slightly larger than the mechanical size of the aperture. This applies to projectors as well as cameras, of course.

Film for titles

The film you use for shooting ordinary subjects is perfectly suitable for titling. Almost invariably this will be colour reversal film, which provides the opportunity to choose a very wide range of colour backgrounds.

Reversal film, of course, is processed to yield the actual projection positive; the film for projection is the same film that was exposed in the camera. This is ideal for amateur use where copies are not normally required. Virtually all Super 8 and standard 8mm camera film is colour reversal.

Colour film is made in two basically different types: daylight and type A, the latter being matched to the much yellower light of the photoflood and movielight class of tungsten filament lamps. Either use the type of film matched to the lighting, or a correction filter to match the film to the light.

Super 8

In the case of Super 8, the manufacturers have simplified everything. They now make only type A film, and the orange 85 conversion filter is built into every Super 8 camera.

When you shoot in daylight the filter is automatically in place for daylight operation, so you do not have to make any special arrangements. However, when you use Super 8 in tungsten light (photofloods, movielights), you have to take the filter out of operation. On most cameras this is done by putting a special key into the movielight slot, or in some cases a screw fitting may be used.

If you were to use a movielight on the camera, the movielight would have the special key built on to it. But an on-camera movielight is not advisable for titling, for two reasons. First, a light directly head-on to the title may give unwanted reflections. And second, if you are shooting titles with the camera pointing vertically downwards, the movielight unit would seriously overheat. Never do this.

Super 8 cameras of the XL (existing light) type generally have their filter operated by a slider switch, marked for daylight (=filter in), and tungsten (=filter out).

Single-8

Users of Fuji Single-8 cameras are in a rather different situation. Film is made in daylight type and tungsten type, with the intention that you use the appropriate film to suit the lighting.

However, the later Single-8 cameras have a built-in filter on a slider control, but note that this is for *tungsten film only*. You *bring in* the filter for daylight usage of the tungsten film. This is the opposite procedure to Super 8, where the filter is already in, and you have to take it out for tungsten lamp shooting. The point about Fuji Single-8 is that you cannot readily use the daylight film for shooting titles indoors with tungsten light. With Super 8 where the 'normal' speed film is the tungsten film anyway, you can just as easily use it indoors in tungsten light simply by taking the filter out of operation.

Daylight film in tungsten light

For the sake of accuracy, it must be said that it is technically possible to use daylight film with tungsten light, but in this case the somewhat deep blue correction filter (80B) is needed to match the very warm light from the lamps to the much more bluish daylight to which the daylight film is naturally balanced. You can use the 80B filter over the lens, but the filter factor is approximately 4-times (ie: two *f* stops). If you have an automatic camera, note the following. First, with the filter over the lens of a TTL metering camera where the cell reads light through the lens, the cell will allow for the filter factor automatically. Second, if the camera is a type with the metering cell in a separate window, you need to put a piece of the blue filter over the cell window *as well* as the main piece of filter over the lens. Third, instead of the latter, if your camera includes manual setting of aperture (full manual override), you set the lens aperture two stops wider than the indicated reading.

With cameras that do not have automatic metering, you simply put the blue filter over the lens and open up the lens aperture by the two *f* stops; two allow for the filter factor.

Remember that for photoflood lamps and movielights (colour temperature nominally 3400 K), the correct filter would be the

Wratten type 80B, while for the very slightly yellower photopearl lamps (3200 K) the correct filter would be the slightly deeper blue 80A.

Lighting your title

Many people think that you cannot make good titles without elaborate equipment. In fact, you can do almost everything you need to do with the simplest equipment and with very little work. Consider the question of lighting.

You can easily film your titles in daylight, if you wish, and if you happen to have a 16mm, Single-8 or standard 8mm camera loaded with daylight film, this is a handy way to use up the last few feet of a roll. With Super 8, which normally uses Type A (indoor) film with built-in filter for daylight shooting, it is equally simple to shoot in daylight (filter in) or in tungsten filament lighting (filter removed).

Daylight has the advantage of being remarkably even, but take care not to cast shadows across the title. Also, daylight in bright weather can be remarkably intense which allows you to shoot at a correspondingly small f stop, and minimizes the effect of any focusing errors.

Tungsten filament lighting, however, has special advantages of its own. First, you can use it at any time, even in the long winter evenings which seem an excellent time to make titles. Tungsten light is controllable so you can readily achieve special effects: spotlight, for example. And it is repeatable, so if you have a standardized set-up you can always give the same exposure (that is, the same f number) for a similar class of title—as long as you standardize your lighting, of course.

Even lighting

The simplest type of lighting—though not always the easiest to achieve—is plain even illumination of a title card. The usual arrangement is to use two lamps, each at 45 degrees to the centre of the title card (*see* p. 59).

Most indoor filming of titles is best done with a reasonably high lighting intensity, so that you are working with the lens moderately well stopped down. This covers a multitude of errors in focusing especially where it proves tricky on this relatively close-up filming.

When placing the classic two lamps at 45 degrees many users make the mistake of placing them too close. They may achieve a good high light intensity, but there could be trouble with surface reflections if you have any sort of gloss on the title card. This is particularly likely if you are using a sheet of cel as an overlay, or even with a sheet of glass for separated background shots.

The geometry for 45 degree lamps shows that each one should be placed *at least* twice the title-width away from the centre of the title.

Naturally you must prevent direct light from the lamps (or from their reflectors) from falling on to the front of the camera lens. Perhaps even more important but less well appreciated, is that if the lamps are even moderately close to the camera, it is advisable to screen off the lamps so that their light and heat do *not* fall on the camera itself. This is most important because plastic-bodied cameras can *melt*, and so will plastic-moulded parts on an otherwise metal-bodied camera.

Filming cels

If you are filming acetate cels for overlays—or even for cartooning (*see* p. 180)—it is absolutely essential that the lights are not reflected from any part of the surface of the cel, when you view it from the camera lens position or through the reflex viewfinder. Reflections from the lamps themselves, and those from their reflectors, must be totally out-of-picture when viewed from the camera lens position.

When shooting cels for cartoon overlays, you will often find that rub marks on the cel will catch the light slightly, even though the lamps are correctly placed to avoid all normal reflections. If you are shooting cartoon material with the cels changed from frame to frame, any such marks will show up as an odd *flashing* at the sides of the picture.

To suppress this problem use crossed polarizers. Place one piece of polarizing sheet over each lamp, both pieces having the

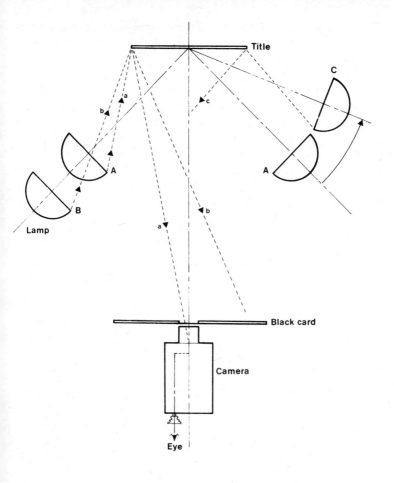

How to avoid reflections. The typical titler with two lamps at 45 degrees to the centre of the title (**A**). If the title has a glossy surface the lamps may reflect from this surface and be visible from the camera lens position. Such unwanted reflections can be avoided by moving the lamps further out to a more acute angle (**B**), or a shallower angle (**C**). It is often necessary to fit a matt black card in front of the camera, with a hole for the lens, to prevent reflections from the camera showing on the glossy title.

polarizing plane in the same direction (eg: vertical), and another piece of polarizing sheet—which must be of good optical quality—over the camera lens and at 90 degrees to the others in polarizing axis.

You can tell when the polarizing direction is correct by looking through the polarizing screen for the camera lens, from the camera position, and with both the lamp polarizers in place. Now if you rotate the camera polarizer, you will see the surface reflection on the cel reach a minimum. This is the correct way round for the camera polarizer.

Using a Titler

If you want to make titles, get a titler. At one time this was essential advice although it is not quite true today.

In the days before through-the-lens reflex viewfinders a titler was necessary to ensure correct line-up of your camera and title. There was also the matter of having the right title size and photographed area.

Equipment designers felt that the best way to achieve correct line-up was to build a titler to suit a particular camera. This was easy in those days, for each of the major manufacturers—and there were very few—had only one or two models of camera.

Pathé and Kodak

Pathé in France made a titler for their 9.5mm Motocamera. Eastman Kodak in the USA made a titler for their 16mm Cine-Kodak. Each of these titlers had a fixed set-up for a particular title size of their choice—a relatively small title area by today's standards. A special supplementary lens was used in front of the camera lens to give good focus on the title.

Pathexgraph titler

In the 1930s the 9.5mm gauge was widely used in Britain and Europe, and 'nine-fivers' could buy the neat little *Pathexgraph* prealigned titler for the Pathescope Motocamera Luxe. The title frame folded down for storage, and the unit was normally used with available light, generally outdoors.

A special supplementary lens was included with the titler, and the camera fitted into a recess giving automatic alignment with the title card. Such a unit could readily be made for almost any camera.

Pathé Titra

Pathé in France also made the *Titra* titler using *back-lit* stencil
type metal letters that fitted into a frame with diffusing glass
and lamp-box behind it. The 50 cm (+2 diopter) supplementary
lens was used over the camera lens.

For simple white-on-black titles this was in many ways an ideal
unit. It is perhaps surprising that the stencil-letter concept has not
been more widely used, though there is the obvious difficulty of
manufacturing letters with a central area that needs support—such
as the letters a, b, d, g, o, p, q. It is worth noting that stencil-type
letters would not be suitable for today's automatic exposure
cameras.

A titler, obviously, is a relatively simple accessory that any small
firm could make. And in the 1930s the world saw the beginning of
titlers made by manufacturers other than those who made the
cameras.

Cinecraft

In Britain, for example, the Cinecraft company began manufacturing a very sensible titler made almost entirely of wood.
This was a notable historical development, for three reasons.
First, it used larger title cards (8 × 6 in) that paved the way to using
felt letters, though the original idea was to draw your own titles
on special sheets of paper with faint blue guide lines that were
supposed not to photograph and generally did not. Second,
Cinecraft made its own lampholders that took standard household
lamps or photofloods. Third, this titler was made in several different
versions, to suit each of the then most popular cameras. Each
had an exactly fitting camera recess for proper location of the
camera in relation to the title holder.

The length of the base—and hence the size of the title—was
designed to use available supplementary lenses, normally 0.5
diopter (50 cm or approximately $19\frac{1}{2}$ in focal length, today generally
known as a 'No 2'). The supplementary was fitted over the camera
lens, and was not part of the titler as on the Kodak model.

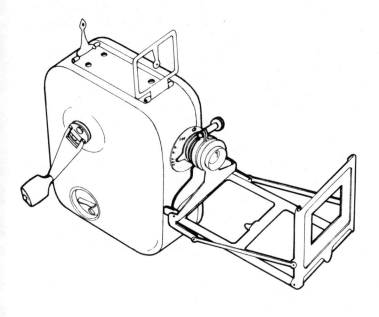

Possibly the world's first-ever amateur titler, this Pathé (France) unit was made for the now historic Pathé Baby hand-turned camera (1923) taking 9.5 mm film. This was introduced just six months before Eastman Kodak launched the first 16 mm in the USA.

The beginnings of 'universal' titlers

By the mid-1930s more cameras were coming on to the market. It soon became no longer practical to make a different model of titler for every camera.

So began the era of the 'universal' titler. Almost any movie camera on its camera platform could be mounted on this titler, but it lost the facility of automatic line-up. This proved to be a great loss for it introduced the need for some skill in setting up. Another disadvantage was that at the end of a titling session, having achieved alignment (usually by making tests on film and developing them in the darkroom) the camera had to be taken off the titler and the whole thing dismantled, thereby losing the alignment so painstakingly set up. Not surprisingly, there were hundreds of so-called universal titlers whose owners never shot a well-aligned title in their lives. For remember, those were the days when almost all movie cameras were non-reflex.

Despite objections, however, universal titlers began to proliferate. The Cinecraft Universal was widely sold, and another version appeared in the 1950s. Names like Wizard and Econasette appeared on the titling scene; the Wizard with felt letters and the Econasign model with well thought-out stencils for lettering. This model also had the supplementary lens held like a lorgnette in front of the camera lens, being supported from the front of the camera platform.

With the advent of universal titlers came the realization that the user could do some special effects fairly easily. So there were soon accessories like horizontal and vertical drums, flip-over title holders, travelling camera platforms for making zoom titles, and others.

Looking back, one sees how even then 16 mm was moving towards the more serious user, and Dallmeyer made a larger titler with a triangular section baseboard (like an optical bench but made of teak), a rectangular 'ring' lighting unit taking eight 60 watt lamps, and a frame taking a metal title board $15\frac{1}{2} \times 11\frac{3}{4}$ in.

Dallmeyer, best known in photographic history as lens manufacturers, did not ignore the amateur market, for they also offered a much smaller and simpler titler with a $9 \times 7\frac{1}{2}$ in metal title board.

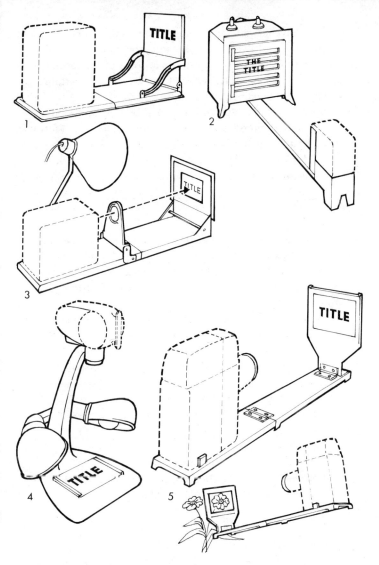

1 The Pathexgraph titler, made for the 9.5 mm Motocamera De Luxe. **2** Pathé Titra, which used stencil letters in front of a lightbox. **3** Cine Kodak titler which included a supplementary lens on a hinged bracket. It did not have its own lighting unit. **4** Bell and Howell 8 mm titler for their early Filmo-8 camera. Lampholders and screening reflectors were an integral part of the prefocused and prealigned design. **5** Later Bell and Howell titler for a standard 8 mm camera. Title frame could be used for close-ups.

With any universal titler you must centre the camera and title with each other, for both height and side-to-side setting. The way you do this depends on the design of a particular titler. For height, some models have an adjustable camera platform, but most have this adjustment on the title board.

Side-to-side centring is usually achieved by having a long crossways slot for the tripod screw in the camera platform. With this, you can fix the camera with the lens central, irrespective of the position of the tripod bush in the bottom of the camera.

Some early movie cameras, almost unbelievably, had no tripod bush. So special titlers had to be made for them with a close-fitting recess to hold the camera. So-called universal titlers were *not* suitable!

Most universal titlers have rails along which the camera carriage can be moved and then locked in the desired working position. This allows you to move the camera up to the title, and most easily adjust height and side-to-side so that the lens and title card are centred one with the other.

When doing this, you should use a card with accurately centred cross-lines drawn on it, and a central circle the size of your lens barrel. You can use this to set the alignment readily. Then you move the camera carriage back to the working distance, set by measuring tape.

You will still have to check and set exactly:

(a)   the sideways 'aim' of the camera (it must point exactly at the centre);

(b)   its vertical aim; and

(c)   that there is no slight tilt, sideways.

Regarding the latter, remember that on some cameras the base is not precisely square to the line of the film; if your camera has this characteristic, you must allow for it.

Using reflex cameras

Nowadays, of course, the majority of cameras have a through-the-lens (TTL) reflex viewfinder, which allows you to see almost exactly the image you will see on the screen when you project the film. Indeed, setting up to film a title on a universal titler is easy and

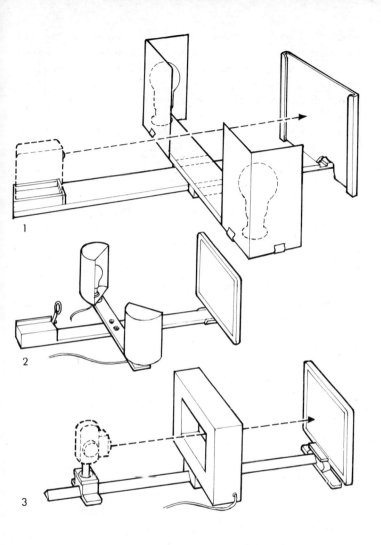

1 Early Cincecraft (UK) titler. The first universal titler, although its wooden 'well' was built to suit one particular camera from a choice of different models.
2 Econasette wooden titler, with a hinged bed to fold up for convenient storage. A supplementary lens holder was fixed to the front of the camera platform. **3** Pre-war Dallmeyer optical bench titler, with holders for camera, lamp unit and title frame which slid to and fro on the teak bed. The lamp unit took eight 60 w lamps and the title board was $15\frac{1}{2} \times 11\frac{3}{4}$ in.

straightforward only if your camera has a reflex finder. The titler has the virtue of being a convenient and fairly well standardized set-up, and a firm one too, on any well made titler. Even with a reflex finder, however, you need to make a viewfinder test (*see* p. 62) to achieve absolute accuracy with your particular camera. Apart from this, lining up a reflex camera is simply a matter of looking through the viewfinder and adjusting the camera and title holder until the alignment looks right. Of course you must focus the camera, generally by using a supplementary lens. This is because most titlers are shorter in length than the minimum focusing distance on most reflex movie cameras. Typically you might use a $+2D$ supplementary lens (No 2, or 50 cm focal length), screwed into the front of the camera lens. The title-to-supplementary distance will be 50 cm ($19\frac{1}{2}$ in), and the zoom lens should be set to infinity focus.

To move in somewhat closer, make use of the focusing scale of the lens, using the figures given on p. 26 for distance and focus setting. You can use the zoom to adjust the photographed width of the title, which is a most convenient arrangement.

HKS titler

Today's breed of universal titler is fairly sophisticated. The 'Rolls Royce' of them all is surely the HKS from West Germany; their TG models are generally regarded as being in the semiprofessional class.

The HKS camera support is adjustable vertically or at an angle, and the carriage moves smoothly forward and back on ground steel rails with a guide rail below. The two twin-lamp lighting units provide a notably even spread of light over the title frame area which is 30×40 cm (12×16 in approximately), and there are sprung card holders and slide-guides. Accessories include an excellent travelling title unit, a friction-roller driven drum, a flip-over plate, and glass title plates.

Because the HKS title frame is quite large, it is readily centred with a tall camera, either a 16 mm model or Super 8 with a long grip below and the tripod socket in the base of the grip. Such cameras may prove a little too high for some smaller universal titlers, which is a point to be watched when buying.

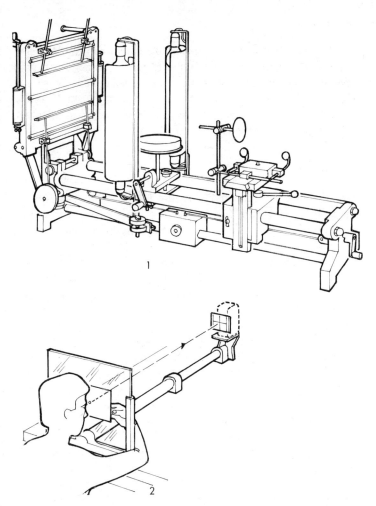

1 The HKS titler, a semi-professional unit from W Germany. The various attachments allow for making almost every conceivable title effect. **2** Presgrip alignment system. A special piece of mirror 3×2 in with crosslines and concentric circles is mounted over the centre of the camera lens. The mirror is held firmly against the front of the lens barrel. A piece of glass or other transparent sheet is used in the title frame, and a centring card held against it. This card has a hole in the centre and crosslines on its front surface. By looking through the back of the card, through the centre hole and to the reflection in the lens mirror the card can be centred.

Malham

Another long-bed titler, less elaborately made than the HKS and costing correspondingly less, is the Malham (Britain), also with several trick-title accessories including travelling title roller unit and a drum. Here again the camera carriage is adjustable to and fro on its long two-rod bed. The title is lit by two lamps in reflectors, and their angles are adjustable.

Muray Titray

Manufactured in the mid-1950s, the French-made Titray was a delightfully neat and practical vertical titler taking cards $3\frac{1}{2}$ in wide, and designed especially for standard 8 mm cameras with screw-in D-mount lenses.

With this unit, the camera fixes to the top plate by unscrewing the lens, taking it off the camera and placing it from below the camera platform, into the $\frac{5}{8}$ in diameter lens hole. You then place the camera on top and screw the lens into the camera body with the thickness of the upper platform between them. The lens hole is of course accurately aligned with the centre of the title holder on the base. So correct alignment is achieved automatically.

The top platform has been carefully counterbored from below to leave the correct thickness (0.025 in) of metal to act as a spacer for the lens. This gives accurate focusing with the standard $\frac{1}{2}$ in or 13 mm lens at the short distance used: approximately $9\frac{1}{2}$ in from the lens flange to the title.

Construction is very simple: two tubular supports up from the base plate hold the top platform. Illumination is by two small round 40 watt lamps in balljoint-mounted deep reflectors that screen the light from the camera lens.

The title frame takes cards approximately $3\frac{1}{2}$ in (90 mm) wide, and the photographed area is roughly $3\frac{1}{8} \times 2\frac{5}{16}$ in. The central part of the title frame is cut out so that the whole unit can be placed over a picture or map which is then filmed through the hole—a neat point. A sheet of ground glass with the titler could be used for projected backgrounds, for example from a slide projector.

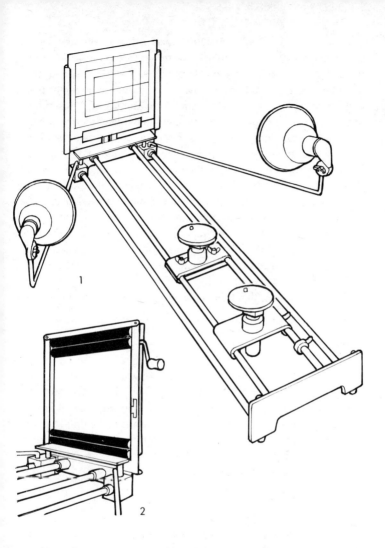

1 Malham Universal Titler. Two separate pairs of rods are used, one pair to hold the end-castings firmly apart and the other pair for the sliding camera platform, and a second platform to hold foreground models, special lenses, or similar attachments. The lamps are in reflectors and easily adjustable. A roller attachment (**2**) permits running titles to be made very simply.

A neat set of $\frac{1}{4}$ in high felt letters was offered with the Titray, and black flock covered plates were provided for simple trick titles: *flap-over title:* end spindles of title plate turn-in spring-clips at either side of the title frame; *swing-in title:* on a quadrant plate with corner spindle that fits into any of the four holes at the corners of the title frame; *flap-up title:* title card held in a clip on a spindle; this fits into bearing holes along one edge of the frame, and the card hinges down into the picture, giving a wipe effect; *running title:* made by pulling the $3\frac{1}{2}$ in wide strip of paper with the title on it, through the frame by attaching the end of the paper to the winding spindle and then turning the handle slowly to pull the paper through the frame as you film.

All these simple effects can readily be applied to a home-built titler. Note, too, that when you have a small and highly portable unit of this type, it can easily be used other than in the vertical position. For example, you could use it outdoors, without the lamps on of course, holding the titler against a flower in the title-frame aperture.

Photax

The long-bed titler is inherently a rather unwieldy thing, and some designs provide for dismantling and storage in a well-made box. Going back again in history, the Photax titler was a well known British model of the 1960 era, with a 36 in long double-rod bed made in two halves that unplugged in the middle. The title frame took cards size $12 \times 9\frac{1}{2}$ in and the camera carriage had a neat sideways tilt adjustment for precise levelling.

Presgrip

Not all titler manufacturers have used double (or triple) rods for their beds. Presgrip used to make a very serviceable titler, neat and sensible as well as being unusually sturdy: a single large-diameter tube, telescoping half-way and fitted with a firm clamp. Here again the unit took sensibly large title cards ($13\frac{7}{8}$ in wide) and— an interesting feature—could be used either horizontally or vertically, the latter by resting it on the title frame.

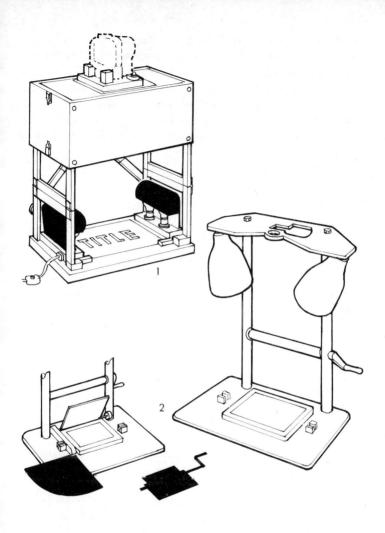

1 The prewar Ensign titler. The camera—usually 16 mm—fitted into a specially made wooden carrier giving correct alignment and positive location. **2** The French Muray was made for 8 mm cameras with interchangeable D-mount lenses. The lens was unscrewed from the camera, fitted through the round hole in the top plate and screwed back into the camera. Attachments were included for flip-over, swing-in, flap-up, and rolling titles.

An adaptor clamp was available for slipping onto the tubular bed, so that the whole thing could be fitted to a tripod. The Presgrip titler was generally supplied without integral lights so had unusually simple and clean lines. Two versions were available, the Standard and the Super, the names *not* referring to film-gauge; the Super had a built-in geared moving title drive with nylon wheels, for a flat Perspex or Plexiglass sheet $13\frac{7}{8}$in wide and as long as desired, 36 in for example. The Super model also had twin lamps, separate from the titler.

Rowi universal titler

Considering that more than 40 years have elapsed since the earliest universal titlers appeared, it is all the more interesting to study a much more recent design: the Rowi 1150 titler from West Germany. Here we have a 60 cm long bed—note the use again of a length based on the No 2 supplementary lens (50 cm)— and the bed is a single tube of relatively large diameter. The The tube is supported at one end by feet below the title frame, and below the neat block that forms the camera platform at the other end. This platform can be adjusted along the tube to alter the camera-to-title distance.

The camera fits on a spigot that clamps into the rear block. You take out the spigot and screw it into the camera which can then be fitted to the titler in a moment. The tripod socket axis is *offset* from the tubular bed.

The cleverest feature is that the whole title frame is adjustable *sideways* over almost all its width. This avoids having to provide any sideways adjustment on the camera platform.

The lamps are mounted on a separate block that also slides to and fro on the bed for distance adjustment, but it also adjusts *sideways,* so that you can set it asymmetrical to the bed but symmetrical to the title-frame so that the lamps line up correctly with the title. This design is novel because almost every other titler is designed to keep the title frame symmetrical to the bed, and then to adjust the camera sideways to keep the optical axis central with the bed.

The title frame is essentially a rectangular 'hoop' of metal, and it

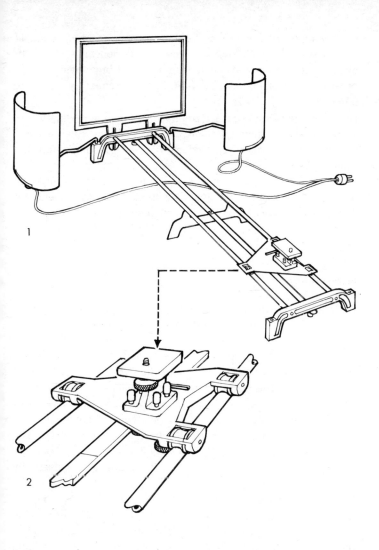

1 The Photax universal titler uses a two-rod bed 36 in long, that divides in half for convenient storage. The camera carriage has three point suspension on rollers (**2**) and a clamp underneath for locking the position. The levelling screws on the camera platform allow for cameras whose base is not exactly level and square with the film-gate. The lamp arms are adjustable.

takes a range of accessories: running title unit, drum, rotatable disc, flap-over and flap-down. This titler is generally used with plastic letters from the same manufacturer, but obviously any other lettering system can be used, such as Letraset, on ordinary title cards.

The lamp unit employs the lamps *end-on,* rather than sideways on, as on so many universal titlers. Reflector lamps can be used. Simple metal shields are provided to screen the lamps from the camera lens.

Note how Rowi accept that the whole point of a 'universal' titler is not just that it will line up with virtually any camera, but that the purchaser of such a titler nowadays may well want to do all the usual trick titles as well. Hence the accent on the various trick-title accessories.

Integral lamps

The question of whether or not a titler should have integral lamps is interesting. With built-in lamps and reflectors the titler is self-contained, even if it sometimes looks like the proverbial Christmas tree with the lighting units 'hung' onto the bed or the title frame. With built-in lampholders and supports, the lamp distance is generally fixed. This means that exposures will always be the same. But on some models the lamps are too close, especially when using a large title card, and do not give even illumination. Also, if you use photoflood type lamps, the heat on the title can be fierce. Most important of all, when filming a cel, or indeed any glossy surfaced title, you are likely to encounter trouble from reflections of the lamps and/or their reflectors.

However, if you use separate lamps to light the title, you can place them where you wish to avoid surface reflections. The light intensity will be less, of course, if the lamps are further away (twice the distance$=\frac{1}{4}$ the light intensity). So compromise and obtain a sensibly small working lens aperture by keeping the lamps reasonably close but carefully placed to avoid surface reflections.

Always remember to screen the lights from the camera lens. The traditional layout of two lamps each at 45 degrees to the title

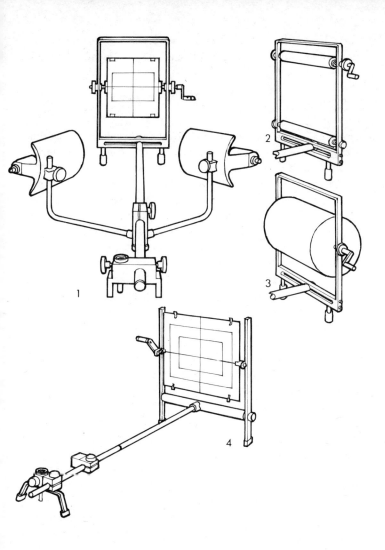

Recent 'universal' titlers such as the West German Rowi (**1**) show noticeable engineering simplification, as well as concentration on front-end accessories such as flap-over plate, rollers (**2**), and drum (**3**). **4** The Susis Model 850, has a flap-over title frame taking a 27 × 23 cm transparent plate and a 70 cm cylindrical bed. Split clamps hold the camera platform and lighting bracket firmly to the bed.

card, is generally best for straightforward titles—unless you want effects lighting, or relief effects with plastic letters throwing shadows.

Medic

One of the interesting changes between the early universal titlers and the more recent ones is that early models were made from wood. Indeed, the early Cinecraft titler was all wood—apart, of course, from the lampholders. Modern universal titlers are all metal, and a typical example is the *Medic* (Switzerland), whose model T16 has a title card format of 24×18 cm, and a base with a stout metal rod on which the cast camera carriage slides to and fro. A second rail is provided to act as a guide to prevent the carriage from swivelling on the main rod.

The same manufacturer makes a smaller model with a single flat base, rather like a simple lathe-bed, and a camera carriage machined to suit. A noteworthy point is that the camera platform has a small piece of angle fixed semipermanently as a guide against which a particular camera can be positioned. This guide is set once and for all by the user, up against the side of the camera after the latter has been properly aligned. Then the camera can be taken off and put back again in exactly the same position. This is a neat arrangement which other manufacturers should copy.

The Medic titlers have the expected good range of accessories, including roller unit for travelling titles, drum and turntable which are smoothly edge-wheel driven, and flip-over transparency frames. The illuminating unit—two reflector lamps on arms—is offered as an accessory and is not required if the titler is to be used only in daylight or with external lamps.

Medic, too, offer a tripod adaptor, a special block for mounting the centre of the bed on a tripod. This is very useful for outdoor work.

Using various cameras

Every one of the professionally made titlers will give ideas that may often be adapted by individual enthusiasts for their own equipment.

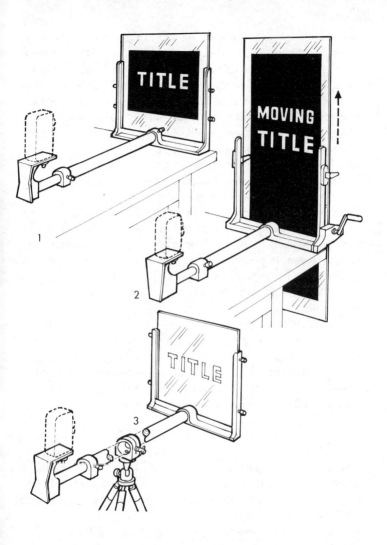

One of the simplest British titlers, the Presgrip. The telescopic bed allows the length to be extended up to 34 in, and the cast title frame has uprights 14 in apart **1** The unit can be used vertically; in this case the title frame acts as the base and gives excellent solidity. **2** More elaborate title frame gives 'running' or rising titles **3** Accessory adaptor clamp allows the bed to be fitted solidly to a tripod.

The interesting aspect of universal titlers nowadays is that there are literally hundreds of different camera models that may have to be used on them. Some cameras are compact, some tall—especially those with an integral grip under the body. Some are reflex, some are not. The cameras may be Super 8, Single 8, which is the same gauge but different shape cartridges and cameras, standard 8 mm, 16 mm, and even perhaps the odd 9.5 mm model among the die-hards who do not like changing gauge.

All this is quite a different concept from the original titlers such as the Kodak and the Pathé, designed to suit one or two particular cameras, and to give automatic line-up with them.

The question of automatic line-up is very significant for any non-reflex camera user. Automatic line-up makes titling so simple that you are likely to use the titler at every available opportunity.

In comparison, it generally needs time to set up a universal titler, as well as care and thought—if not sheer skill—in lining up a non-reflex camera with the title card. This applies especially to the beginner.

So if you plan to make titles on a non-reflex camera and are setting out specifically to buy a universal titler, you should look for one that enables you to return readily to the same settings every time you use the outfit. However, a camera with a reflex viewfinder eliminates the need to work almost 'blind' (non-reflex), as you can see in a reflex viewfinder almost exactly what you will photograph.

Inevitably one has the feeling that many universal titlers are so flexible, with a wide range of movements and adjustments, that they will suit any and every camera. But the very flexibility of adjustment means that the entire thing must be set up afresh every time it is used, for usually the settings are lost when you take the titler apart again for storage.

With a non-reflex camera there is a lot to be said for a titler that suits the particular camera and gives automatic line-up. On the other hand, today's rate of camera obsolescence is such that most models are likely to be superseded after a mere couple of years. So a title unit made to suit one camera is likely to be left on the dealer's shelf, and to be disastrous for the company making it.

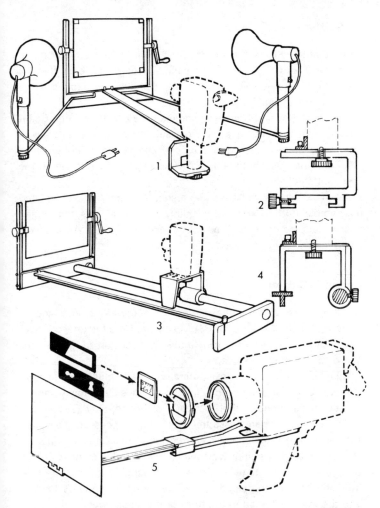

1 The Swiss Medic T8 titler uses a fixed-distance bed consisting of a T-section bar. Title size is 13×18 cm. **2** Medic T16 has a 18×24 cm title and adjustable camera carriage, with a lock-screw to fix it. A pre-set angle strip ensures that the camera can be put on the platform in the same position every time. **3** 8 mm Medic with a bed consisting of a round rod to give positive alignment of camera carriage (**4**). **5** The Austrian Eumig Macro Set, made for specific cameras, such as the PMA 880. The simple bed clips into the base of the camera. The supplementary lens fits over the zoom lens.

Instatitler

The Instatitler S8, is a neat little unit from West Germany made specifically for Kodak's first two simple Super 8 cameras, the M2 and the M4. The very simplicity of this titler gives ideas to the do-it-yourself enthusiast.

The camera platform holds the camera in line with the title board which is on the end of a twin-rail support arm. The rails are in effect side-plates that continue up over the camera to hold a small reflector type household lamp which is angled down to aim at the title centre.

A set of self-adhesive letters and a supplementary lens completed this simple outfit. 'Never was titling so simple' was the slogan of the manufacturers, and they were absolutely right. An easy-to-use titler is likely to be *used*.

Canon 318 titler

Another small titler for one particular camera has been made by Canon for their neat little XL-318M camera. Here the titler attaches by supporting arms to the top (movielight) socket of the camera, and external lighting is used.

Frankly, if you have a reflex camera, you have much less need of a titler because you can readily line up on titles by simply using the camera on a tripod, either vertically or horizontally (*see* p. 58). If, however, you wish to use the various trick accessories available for the universal titlers, such as travelling titles, drums, flap-over, etc., you may find a titler worthwhile with a reflex camera.

One of the most interesting ideas is to support a miniature titler from the front of the camera lens. This is easily done by fixing it into the internal thread in the front of the lens barrel.

Pocket titler

Such an arrangement is most readily applied to a non-zoom lens because a suitably strong supplementary lens can be used for the close distance, without insuperable optical problems encountered with some zooms. The outstanding example of this concept

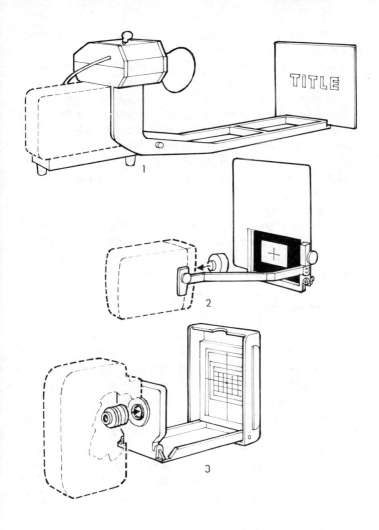

Top Instatitler, made for the Kodak M2 and M4. An integral-reflector lamp illuminates the title. **Centre** Elmo Pocketauto for standard 8mm film. The supplementary lens is plugged into the front of the fixed-focus camera lens. The plate around the title is mid-grey and reflects the incident light back to the CdS cell for non-TTL metering. **Bottom** Malham Compact titler, made from basically a 6×6cm slide viewer. The viewer lens screws into the camera lens.

is the *Malham Coil 70 Pocket Titler,* a neat unit that folds up into about the size of a cigarette packet.

This small titler is in fact adapted from the *Coil Seventy* viewer for 7×7 cm slides. The photographed area is relatively quite small and centred with the lens, of course. The supplementary lens is built into the screw mount that fits into the camera lens. The whole unit swivels so that you can keep the title itself level with the camera when filming. The title distance is only 100 mm (just under 4 in), and the unit is used with external lighting. Titles are made by Letraset on to 6×6 cm pieces of card, or transparent coloured pieces of cel if desired, in which case you use black Letraset and back-light the title.

A camera with an interchangeable non-zoom lens has an advantage over a zoom in one respect. You can shim the lens out a little, to focus it on a close-up distance, and thus avoid the need for a supplementary lens.

Eumig Macro Set

The concept of a simple title-holder arm supported from the front of a camera itself is attractive especially if it can be done neatly. A delightful example made by Eumig (Austria) is part of a so-called *Macro Set.* Here an arm fits into the specially shaped front of the PMA camera models, and a special supplementary lens (supplied in the set) is fitted to the front of the camera lens. The title card is fitted into the outer end of the arm. The title distance is 12 in from the film-plane mark (5.88 in from the supplementary lens). As with any reflex camera, you can see the line-up in the viewfinder. The minimum width of the title depends on the focal length setting of the camera's zoom lens.

Vertical titlers

It is an advantage to have your title card lying horizontally when you are using loose letters, so a vertical titler is a great help here, as well as for animation and cartooning where you have to do a lot of the work on the title card plane.

Over the years there have not been many titlers made specifically for vertical operation. History records that the original French Pathé 9.5 mm titler was a miniature vertical model, and Muray made one in the 1950s. Apart from these, the only notable vertical titler appeared in the early 1930s, and that was from an interesting British firm that now seems to have vanished without trace: Ensign.

Ensign vertical titler

Ensign's *Animator and Titler* was cleverly designed to fold up into a storage box which was about one-third the height of the assembled unit and formed the top part of it. The camera lay in a cradle in the top, and the cradle panels were interchangeable to suit different cameras. The title size was $10 \times 7\frac{1}{2}$ in and sets of felt letters were supplied.

The home constructor will immediately see possibilities for making a vertical titler. Remember that the camera must be the same way up as your title card. That is, the base of the camera should be the same side as the *bottom* of the title card, otherwise your title will project upside-down on the screen.

Vertical rostrums

Vertical titlers tend to be less flexible than horizontal ones where special effects are concerned. But as almost all professional titles are shot on a vertical camera 'rostrum', it becomes apparent that the flexibility or otherwise is mainly a matter of design.

Some amateur titlers such as the *Presgrip* can be used equally well either horizontally or vertically. In the vertical mode the title frame acts as the base that will stand firmly on a workbench.

Many photographic enlargers can also be used as a vertical copy-stand or titler. Sometimes you do this by taking off the complete enlarger head and putting on a separate arm, sold as an accessory, that fits on the upright column. With some enlargers, you can take off the enlarger unit and fit a flat base to the supporting bracket. Enlargers have the advantage of being adjustable for height, that is, camera-to-title distance.

When planning a vertical titler, you can obviously design-in features you require, such as a glass platform for the title letters or cels, with a separately lit background a short distance below it.

Standardized set-up

The advantage of using a titler is that it gives a standardized set-up which makes it easier to shoot a standardized form of title card. With a non-reflex camera, a titler with positively repeatable location for the camera is invaluable. On the other hand, with reflex viewfinding, you can do most forms of titling just as well with a firm tripod and separate lamps.

With almost any titler, remember your camera-to-title distance will be less than the minimum focusing distance on many cameras. On some models of camera you can use the *macro* setting for closer focusing, but this is sometimes inconvenient for title size and distance as well as difficult to focus reliably in the viewfinder. It is almost always better, therefore, to add a supplementary lens over the camera lens (*see* p. 26), so that you still have the use of the zoom for size adjustment without having to move the camera carriage to and fro.

If, however, you are working with a non-zoom camera, you obviously have to move the camera to and fro for size adjustment and then focus accordingly. Normally it is simpler to make the title cards the right size for filming on a fixed camera distance.

A home-made titler

Any home handyman can make a very serviceable titler for routine filming of title cards of a standardized size. The special point of this design is that the camera can be taken off and later put back again in exactly the same alignment. This is obviously especially well suited to non-reflex cameras, because you only have to go through the aligning and testing operation once. The drawings show the layout, and the dimensions can be modified to suit any camera. The first part to be designed is the camera platform, and the idea is that the camera should locate into the corner of an L-shaped raised edge at the front and along one side (the opposite side to the camera door).

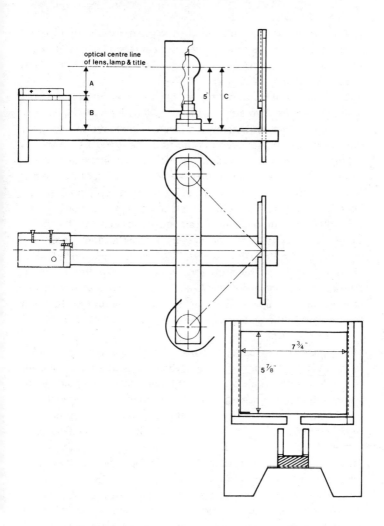

The basic construction of a home-made wooden titler for 8×6 in title cards. The platform must support the camera so that the lens axis is central with the title frame. An L-shaped location is screwed to the platform to fit the camera. $\frac{1}{4}$ in Whitworth grub screws are used to make final adjustment to the camera position.

The camera baseplate can be made of plywood about $\frac{3}{8}$ in (10 mm) thick, of a size to suit your particular camera, plus raised edges on the front and one side. These edges can be about $\frac{1}{2}$ in (12 mm) wide and about $\frac{3}{4}$ in (20 mm) high.

Although it would be possible simply to locate the camera into the corner of the L, it is better to use true three-point adjustment, by putting in three grub-screws: one at the front and two along the side. These can be screwed into holes in the wood, as shown, by drilling the holes for them slightly under the nominal size and then tapping the wood with a metal-working tap, to form proper screw-threads. In the original titler, $\frac{1}{4}$ in Whitworth grub screws were used (the same thread as a standard camera tripod socket), and Allen-type grub screws were obtained from an engineers' stores, together with the neccessary Allen (hexagon form) key with which to turn the screws. The holes were drilled $\frac{7}{32}$ in, ready for tapping. The grub screws are set to protrude slightly through to the inside of the L-shaped part, so that the camera rests against the tips of the screws and can be located by them. In due course, the screws can be sealed with a blob of adhesive, to fix their positions.

The camera having being approximately positioned on the platform, a piece of thin, ribbed rubber matting was stuck to the top of the platform. This is to prevent the camera slipping about, without it being necessary to do up the fixing screw unduly tightly into the tripod bush. Note that the rubber should be stuck only on the part of the platform immediately below the base of the camera itself, leaving the door overhanging the edge of the rubber. This allows the camera door to be opened without having to disturb the camera position.

The hole for the fixing screw should be drilled in the base of the platform, after the camera has been lined up as closely as possible to the expected final position. The grub screws are adjusted so that they rest against the camera body. The hole for the fixing screw may be made appreciably larger than the screw itself— that is, larger than the normal $\frac{3}{4}$ in clearance hole you might expect to use, so that it does not interfere with the setting against the three grub screws which provide the exact location when the camera is being put on. The fixing screw can be made by cutting a $\frac{1}{4}$ in wing screw to the appropriate length to go through the wood, which protrudes by exactly the right amount into the camera tripod socket, then a large washer can be added. This holds the camera on the platform.

The next step is to make the main bed of the titler, then to support the camera platform on it at the right height. In the original titler, the main bed was made of $2\frac{1}{2} \times \frac{3}{4}$ in (finished) wood and the length was 27 in—though the latter might need to be slightly longer if your camera is particularly long between the front of the lens, and the rear end of the camera body. The titler was designed around the concept of using a +2 dioptre supplementary over the camera lens, and so having a supplementary-to-title distance of $19\frac{1}{2}$ in ($\frac{1}{2}$ m). The overall length of the main bed can be left longer than required, and may be cut down last of all, after the line-up procedure has been completed.

The original titler was designed to use a title card 8×6 in overall. The photographed area is of course considerably less.

The height of the camera platform is set primarily by the height of the lamps, which of course are matched to the height of the centre-line of the title. The lamps are 5 in (125 mm) from the base of their batten-type holders, to the centre-line of the widest part, from where the light is mainly emitted. Lamps of 100 w rating are used. These are about the same size as No 1 Photofloods, which can be used if a lot of light is needed for a particular job.

The lampholders are fixed to a crossbar of $2\frac{1}{2} \times \frac{3}{4}$ in (finished) wood, approximately 18 in long. The drawing shows the lamps at 45 degrees to the centre of the title, but in practice it is advisable to position them slightly further out. This prevents any reflection in the edges of the title, when a glossy title is being used.

The whole titler rests on three 'feet', one at the rear end of the camera platform, and two which are the under-part of the title frame. The title frame is made from a piece of $\frac{3}{8}$ in (10 mm) plywood, $12\frac{1}{4} \times 10$ in (310 × 254 mm) square. The centre of the title comes $5\frac{3}{4}$ in (120 mm) above the top of the main bed, $\frac{3}{4}$ in (20 mm) thick. 2 in (50 mm) was allowed below the bed for the supporting feet.

This brings the centre-line of the title $8\frac{1}{2}$ in (215 mm) above the bottom edge of the plywood. The wood is carefully cut away to form a snug fit on the main bed. This allows the title frame to be readily slid to and fro along the title bed to get final adjustment of distance. The frame is finally fixed in place with two angle-brackets about 2×2 in (50×50 mm). It is easiest to fix these angles to the frame only at first, and to add a flat strip screwed from side to side of the title holder, just below the main bed, tentatively holding the title frame to the bed but leaving it easily adjustable along the bed.

It is a good idea to have a hole right through the title frame, so that objects can be placed behind it, for example to form a background, and lettering can be put on glass in the title frame. Make the hole approximately $7\frac{3}{4} \times 5\frac{7}{8}$ in (200×150 mm), through plywood on the same centre-lines as the title card itself (ie at the stated height, and centrally across the width of the frame).

Note that the optical axis of the camera lens is kept on the centre-line of the whole titler and the title card.

The front of the plywood title holder has retaining pieces into which the title card can be slid. The retaining slots are made by using L-section beading, fitted as strips at either side of the card, and overlapping its side edges by about $\frac{1}{8}$ in (3 mm), to retain it. At the bottom edge of the title card, a plain wooden strip is used as a stop on which the card can rest; cut away a 1 in (25 mm) section in the centre as a finger-slot for pushing the card up and out. The bottom strip should be only lightly fixed at first; it may be necessary to move it slightly up or down for final adjustment of the title height.

Reverting to the crossbar carrying the lampholders, the two lampholders are wired up and fitted with a suitable plug for the mains. The two lamps are of course wired in parallel.

Reflectors can be made from round tins approximately $4\frac{1}{4}$ in (105 mm) diameter and 7 in (175 mm) high. Each tin should be carefully cut with snips down the front, an angle of about 135 degrees being cut right out. The cut sides nearest the centre of the titler can be bent slightly outwards, so that they cannot mask the light from the opposite edge of the title. Note that these side-flaps screen the bulbs from the lens.

The crossbar carrying the lamps is fixed to the main bed, at a distance of approximately $5\frac{1}{2}$ in from the title holder to the front of the lamp crossbar. However, it is best not to fix this position until you have viewed a shiny title from the camera position and checked that there are no reflections from the lamps and reflectors appearing at the edge of the title. If there are any reflections, move the lamps in a little closer until the reflections disappear. For easy dismantling for storage, the lamp crossbar can be fixed to the main bed by a single $\frac{1}{4}$ in Whit. (or 6 mm) bolt about 2 in (50 mm) long. This can be taken out for dismantling, and held firm with a wing-nut and washer when in use.

When construction is complete, the whole of the wooden structure can be stained black, and the outsides of the tin reflectors painted black with a heat-resisting paint. Cut a hole in the bottom of each can to suit the lampholder used.

The camera can be aligned exactly with the centre of the title card, by a mixture of judgement and test exposures of a few frames. The three grub screws can be adjusted as required, especially the two side screws which aim the camera for the correct side-to-side centring. Thereafter, the camera can be taken off and put back in exactly the same position.

Note that Super 8 cameras, which generally load from the right-hand side, need their locating L-shaped piece to be as shown in the diagram. But in the case of standard 8 mm cameras, the door is on the left side and the L-shaped locating piece should, therefore, be on the opposite side. The same applies to 16 mm cameras, which may need greater height for the title and lamps, to cope with the greater height of the lens centre-line.

Title size

When you choose a titler, you commit yourself to a particular size of title card. On the other hand, your lettering system itself largely decides the desirable size of title card. Thus, if you use Letraset, you will probably want a reasonably large typeface, because it is easier to achieve an appearance of good alignment. True, Letraset is also available in very small sizes, but then you need to take extra care in setting out.

If you wish to use loose letters, moulded plastic for example, you will find them available mostly in the larger typefaces, again requiring fairly large title cards.

Yet there is considerable attraction in using a small and compact titler. The original Cine-Kodak titler had the right idea in this respect, with a title holder opening $3\frac{5}{8} \times 2\frac{3}{4}$ in, in which the type had to be kept certainly no wider than $2\frac{1}{2}$ in.

The American cine magazine *Home Movies* (no relation of the 1930s British magazine of the same name) every month used to print a page of ready-to-shoot titles, each size $3 \times 2\frac{1}{4}$ in overall. Unfortunately many were designed with the wording or design overflowing the photographed area, for the artists had not appreciated how important it is to have plenty of space around the wording and design, to avoid either cutting off some of it, or alternatively of having the edges in-picture.

Guide 'rules' for width of lettering, photographed area, and size of card, are given on p. 28.

Special Effects Lighting

Not every title has to be flat lit, that is, evenly lit all over, for with a little ingenuity you can use your lighting to give special effects. Take a simple title card with white lettering on a medium-dark grey (*not* black) background and imagine you have a spotlight.

Spotlighting

Now obviously you could use the spotlight to throw a beam of light on to the title card, narrowing the beam until you light just the important centre of the title. Or you could throw the light across the title in a big diagonal V, probably from the lefthand top corner because this generally seems the most natural direction for those of us who are brought up to expect light from above and to read from left to right. Another interesting possibility is to use colour, perhaps by putting a sheet of colour filter material over your spotlight, to give a coloured beam.

If you do not have a photo-spotlamp you may have, or be able to borrow, a 2×2in slide projector, without slides in it, of course. A slide projector makes a useful and efficient spotlamp for titling, and the beam can be sharp-edged or soft, according to how you focus the lens. You can also make cut-out masks to go in the slide-carrier to control the beam, or even to throw interesting patterns such as a window or venetian blind.

Relief effects

Spotlighting comes into its own with relief lettering. When you use moulded plastic title letters, you can readily obtain some fine relief effects by using a slanting beam from a spot. By adjusting the position of the spot in relation to the title, you can modify the appearance of the shadows cast by the lettering.

Generally the relief effect looks best if the light comes from top left of the title, because the wording is most easily read with the shadows below and following the letters. But this is a matter of taste, and you can experiment with the spotlamp in different positions. With a reflex camera, study the effect in the viewfinder and see exactly how the title looks with any particular lighting. If you use a non-reflex camera, study the effect of the lighting by looking at the title as near as possible from the camera lens position. Do not be afraid to experiment with the spotlamp. Move it around boldly and study the effect in the viewfinder until you find the most appropriate position of the lamp for the effect you want.

Vary the effect on relief lettering by using either a soft or a hard spot. A focused slide projector beam will give very sharp-edged shadows from the letters. A floodlamp, pressed into service as a makeshift 'spot' will give quite soft-edged shadows. A 500–1000 watt photo spot with Fresnel lens (a *pup*, in film-studio parlance) will give medium-soft edged shadows and an excellent relief effect. You can soften the shadows by adding some relatively soft (large-source) light; this reduces the depth of the shadows by putting some light into the shadow areas. Do this with relatively large-source lights, or even with light bounced from a large sheet of white card, otherwise you risk getting double-shadows which would spoil the attractive relief effect on the lettering.

When placing the lamps, you must always locate each one where it will not cause any surface reflections if anything shiny is included in the title, for example, glossy letters, cels, glass.

Glass shots

One of the most useful title effects is to separate the lettering from the background, having the lettering on glass and the background separately lit some distance behind it. The distance between the two must be sufficient to avoid shadows from the lettering from falling on the background.

By having a reasonable distance between the title letters on the glass and the background, you can light the background separately. You may care to use effects lighting such as a spot on to the background (*see* p. 5, colour plates).

Top left: Presgrip letters (UK) are available in several typefaces and sizes, upper and lower case.

Top right: Wurker letters (W Germany) are made in white plastic with coloured face if required. Blue works well on an orange background.

Centre left and right: Background colours create different effects and moods but avoid very bright colours. Subdued colours work best with white letters.

Bottom left: Elaborate titles need letters that can be fixed in position. Vacuum, magnetic and self-adhesive are the three main methods.

Bottom right: China clay letters (Hernard, USA) have an excellent matt white surface but are fragile.

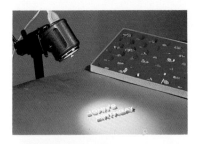

Top left: A small angled spotlight gives excellent relief effects.

Top right: An angled floodlight gives a softer effect.

Centre left: Felt letters are held on flock or velvet. Moulded plastic 'tree' letters are relatively inexpensive.

Centre right: A border looks attractive but needs careful lining-up.

Bottom left: Many titlers can also be used for close-up work.

Bottom right: Faded etchings make useful backgrounds for plastic letters.

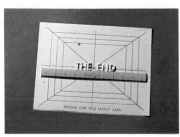 

Top left: Magnetic letters have tiny magnets which adhere to a steel plate behind the background.

Top right: For most titles, plain white letters are best, but coloured fronts can sometimes be useful.

Centre left: Letraset type letters are rubbed down into place on a title card, by pressure on the backing sheet.

Centre right: Magnetic letters adhere well to the steel plate behind the thin background paper.

Bottom left: Plastic letters are set along a ruler, laid upon the transparent plastic backing sheet, behind which the alignment and centring sheet can be used.

Bottom right: Different styles of letter give different relief effects, with suitable spotlighting. Note the different relief with the straight-sided Hernard letters and the chamfered Presgrip.

Separate lighting for title letters (on glass) and the background which is some distance away. Two spotlights can be used, but one spot and one flood are satisfactory. A slide projector can be used as a spotlight.

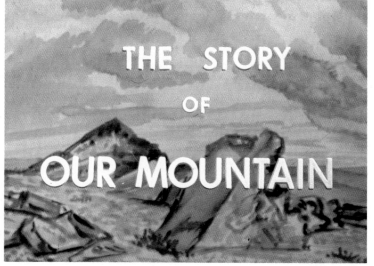

Top: Background lighting is increased to give black lettering on the picture background.

Bottom: The level of lighting on the white lettering is arranged to give good emphasis against the background on which the lighting is subdued.

Above: Animation cels are photographed one at a time, but here eight cels have been superimposed to show the effect of movement. The background is a separate painting. *Original cels by Valerie Ellis.*

Opposite: Animation cels, much reduced to show the stages in a horse and rider walking across the picture.

Bottom left: The effect of cel No 7 against the background. All the original cels were of course punched with register holes to fit on the pin bar when photographed. *Original cels by Valerie Ellis.*

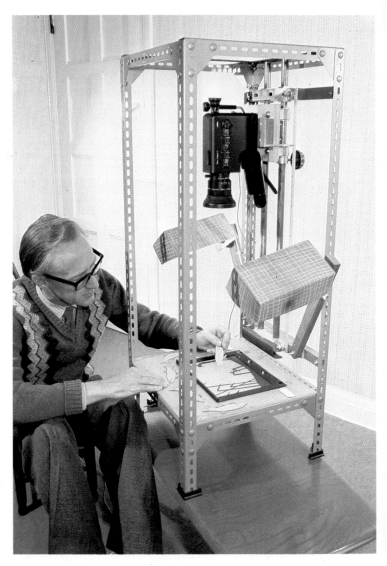

This simple animation rostrum is being used here by its designer, Alan Cleave. The rostrum is built from slotted angled dexion, with the camera carriage of $\frac{3}{4}$in bearings sliding on $\frac{3}{4}$in rods. For constructional simplicity the camera is mounted base away from the user.

Remember that the background may have to be larger—perhaps very much larger—than the photographed title area on the glass. The greater the separation, the larger the background will need to be. For example, if the lettering area on the glass were to be 20 in (50 cm) from the camera lens, and the background 40 in (100 cm) away, the background area would need to be twice as wide as the lettering area. In practice you will not use as much separation as in this example, but always be sure to have the background large enough so that you never have the edges in-picture.

The most convenient layout is to have the camera pointing vertically downwards, and the glass platform for the lettering held by supports at either side. Then the background below it can be lit by slanting light without obstruction from the supports.

You will find plenty of scope for creative ingenuity with lighting on the separate background, and indeed with selecting the background itself. Many textured materials such as canvas and some wallpapers will make excellent backgrounds, especially when lit with a spotlamp from a glancing angle that emphasizes the texture. With this sort of arrangement you will generally have evenly lit lettering with spotlit background, and this means the separation between lettering and background must be sufficient for the even light on the lettering not to affect the background appreciably. When executed well, this can give highly effective titles.

When several titles are used in succession in a film, it is necessary to change the title lettering (on the glass), but to leave the background and its lighting *exactly the same.*

Using cels

The title lettering can either be actually on the glass itself (convenient if using plastic letters) or on cels laid on the glass. Using the cels is convenient when making several titles in succession, especially if the wording is elaborate. If the cels curl or bulge up, they may have to be held flat under a sheet of glass. When using glass—with or without cels—take care to place the lamps so that there will be no surface reflections from it.

When several titles on cels are being shot in succession, you should pre-align each, either making position marks, or using punched register holes and a pin-bar (*see* p. 177). The shooting session will go much more smoothly than if you had to align each title in the viewfinder by eye. But if only two or three titles are being taken, it may be simpler to set them up by eye in between shooting the required length of each title.

Tricks with Titles

You can have plenty of fun with trick titles, especially if the tricks leave your audience wondering how they were done. But remember that they should always have some relevance to the title for which they are used.

Single-frame shooting

Simplest of all, perhaps, is *single-frame animation*. By exposing one frame at a time, you can move your title letters slightly between each frame, and make them appear to slide into place as the title proceeds.

Animating even a simple title needs patience. Assume you are using Super 8 film with a normal projection speed of 18 fps (normal speed for Super 8 and Single 8), and you want a 10 second title. This means 180 frames of film. If you use the first six seconds to move the letters in, and the final four seconds with the title completed and static on the screen, you still have to shoot $6 \times 18 = 108$ frames. Now suppose the title consists of only four words made up of 20 characters. Each of the 20 letters will have to be moved a little between each frame which represents $108 \times 20 = 2160$ moves of individual letters—all for six seconds of screen-time. It certainly needs patience though the work can be reduced by careful planning. You might, for example, move the letters only every other frame without the difference being really notice-able—but it halves the effort.

Despite the often fantastic amount of work, single-frame animation is fascinating and rewarding, especially when done carefully and skilfully. Begin by making a few tests with, say, plastic letters when you have a few feet of film to use up at the end of a roll. Plan a title with the letters coming into place or, as is more usual, the words being spelled out one letter at a time. For the latter you will want the letters to appear at intervals of $\frac{1}{3}$ sec, and in this case you would shoot 6 frames per letter, for 18 fps projection, or 8 frames per letter for 24 fps projection. Allow a longer interval at the end of each word, about 12 and 16 frames for 18 and 24 fps projection, respectively.

Choose an appropriate subject for this 'spelling out' title and you will be surprised how effective it can be.

As with most tricks, ingenuity is important. You will find many interesting ideas springing to mind once you have the feeling for what you can do with single-frame animation (*see* p. 178).

Cameras for single-frame operation

If you plan to do much single-frame work, you must choose a camera with a built-in electro-magnetic release. In conjunction with the single-frame facility which is found on most silent cameras (though relatively few sound models), electro-magnetic releasing will enable you to expose one frame at a time *by remote control.* You need only add an accessory switch-button on the end of a cable that can be plugged into the remote control socket on the camera.

This has two great advantages. First, you can expose each frame with a touch on the remote switch-button—a simple microswitch, for example—and thus completely avoid touching and perhaps jarring the camera every time you want to expose a frame. Second, you can place your remote control switch-button alongside the subject you are animating, so you do not have to get up to reach the camera for every frame.

When shooting single-frame animation, be sure your camera is fixed *absolutely firmly* to its support. Even the slightest movement of the camera will ruin the essential smooth effect of animation.

Particularly with cameras where you have to give the release itself a good hard press for a single-frame exposure, you must have the camera on a really firm support. Many ordinary tripods are quite inadequate for this application.

Cameras without electro-magnetic releasing can often be used with a cable-release, and a suitably long release helps to reduce

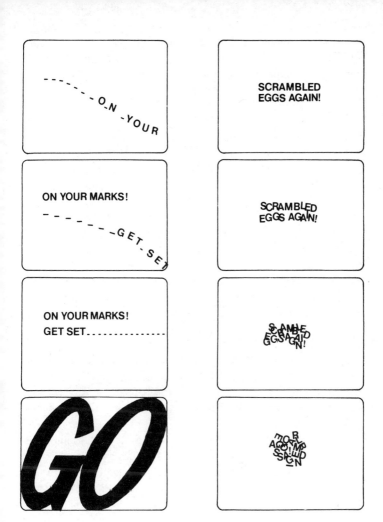

Left Single frame shooting for titles. This example shows letters moving on the screen to give the idea of action. **Right** A title idea showing the use of reverse action. This effect is only possible using 16 mm.

the chance of moving the camera when you make each exposure. By holding the cable-release in a gentle curve you can avoid camera movement when pressing the release.

Reverse action

To be able to shoot a title in reverse to the way in which it will be projected is a useful facility for certain titling tricks. Specifically, it is most useful when you want the title to begin with jumbled letters that 'sort themselves out' (by single-frame animation, usually) into neat rows of letters forming the title.

This effect is easier to achieve if you can do it in reverse: to start shooting with the title wording impeccably laid out, then step by step to move the letters into a jumble, over a few seconds of screen-time.

With some cameras this is simple. With others it is impossible. You can do reverse-action shooting on 16 mm very easily, if you use double-perforation film, and simply have the camera *upside-down* in relation to the title (or more easily, have the title upside-down in relation to the camera).

Naturally, when you project this processed film, the title will appear upside-down. So cut it out of the film, reverse it end-to-end, and resplice it into the roll. When you project it, the title will appear the right way up, but the last end you shot will be shown first. Reverse action!

You can only do this on 16 mm because double-perforation film is symmetrical, and will therefore project equally well end-first.

The non-symmetrical format films, however, will not permit this turning around for reverse action. Fuji Single-8, Super 8, standard 8 mm and single-perforation 16 mm cannot be reversed in this way, and with these gauges there is no simple way you can film in reverse.

Even one or two standard 8 mm cameras that would *run* in reverse (the Elmo TL6 and TL4, for example) cannot be used for reverse single-frame shooting because the camera's single-frame stop-pawl was only designed for forwards operation. And even with 16 mm single-perforation film on those cameras that will do single-frames in reverse (after having run the desired length of film through forwards with the lens cap on) there is inevitably a slight change of frame-line position that would need reframing on the projector for that shot only every time you project the film.

Travelling titles

When you have a lot of words to put into one title, such as a long cast list, you naturally do not want the wording to be too small so as to be unreadable. One of the answers to this problem is the travelling, creeping, or rolling title, with the wording on a long length of paper or card, pulled slowly but smoothly through the title frame as the camera is running.

Remember that this sort of title is only appropriate when the length of your wording would fill *more than two* static titles, in depth. If you were to make a travelling title which only had to move a little to include the bottom lines, it would look wrong. So the travelling title should be used when you have enough lines of words to fill at least $2\frac{1}{2}$ times the depth of the normal photographed area.

Now a word about the speed of travel. The idea is that you should 'roll' the title upwards at approximately the same speed that the average viewer reads the words. If anything, you should move the title faster, rather than slower, so that you are 'pacing' the reader. This is better than going at a snail's pace so that the audience is waiting for the next line to come into view.

Therefore you will have to adjust the speed of travel so that it looks right on the screen. This depends, of course, on the number of words to a line, and the sort of words they are. People's names, for example, take slightly longer to assimilate than simple words conveying some fact.

Let us take an example. Suppose your photographed area is 8×6 in. This may well be on a card or roll of paper 12 in wide. If you work in metric sizes, this is about 20×15 cm photographed area, on a card 30 cm wide. For an average title of the sort you may need to 'travel', you will need to move it upwards at a rate corresponding to the title height (photographed height) in something like 6 to 12 seconds. This means you need a speed of travel of something like $\frac{1}{2}$ to 1 in per sec for this title size.

Drum titles

The easiest way to make travelling titles is not with title cards or rolls, but with a 'drum' fixed in the title frame. The drum surface should be roughly level with the plane normally occupied by a title card. The title is then laid out around the drum which is slowly turned as the camera is running. Pivots for the drum are readily made, and the ingenious moviemaker will be able to arrange a suitable drum by adapting a large round tin, and adding pivots or a spindle exactly centrally.

Most drums made for titling are far too small. You need a circumference at least four times the photographed height of the title. The circumference of the drum will be π (3.14) times the diameter. You need plenty of 'length' around the circumference, so that you run no risk of spilling over on to the part of the title with which you started, should you turn the drum too far if the end is close to the beginning when the title is wrapped around the drum.

There are several ways to use lettering on a drum. One is to stick black flock paper or black velvet around the drum. This enables you to use light felt letters which adhere quite well.

A little more sophisticated, perhaps, is to paint the drum matt black, and then use magnetic letters which will cling to a 'tinplate' drum. You will of course need the smaller sizes of magnetic letters, to avoid needing an unwieldy drum (*see* p. 46).

Stick-on letters may also be used on a painted drum, but be prepared to touch up the matt black surface when necessary because new 'tacky' letters are strongly adhesive and they often pull the paint away when you pull off the letters.

If you have a reflex viewfinder on your camera, you can have the title drum rigged up on a simple stand with pivots for the drum to be turned by a handle on the end. The drum does not need to be part of an elaborate titler.

Simply set up your camera so that the photographed area will be well inside the edges of the drum. It should be accurately lined up with the centre spindle as regards height, and aligned with the middle of the drum for side-to-side setting.

The most professional titles are made by using either printed (or photo-set) lettering or carefully laid out Letraset type lettering.

This is perfectly practical, and typically you would make the title on a piece of background paper the same width as the drum and its circumference in length. This scroll of paper with the title on it can then be fixed carefully to the drum using adhesive tape at the join between start and finish of the roll of paper and, if need be, around the extreme edge here and there, well outside the photographed area. Alternatively, double-sided tape can be used.

There are many ready-made titlers on the market with title drums provided. Most of these drums are far too small in diameter and give a distressing effect on the screen by moving the lettering closer (hence increasing in size) at the centre of the screen, and decreasing in size again as it moves down. A large drum minimizes this effect.

Travelling card titles

Filming a flat title, pulled smoothly through the title frame, is the usual method of making a travelling title. If you only wish to make titles of this sort occasionally, it is not worth making or buying elaborate equipment, although you have to do *something* to move a title smoothly past your camera lens as you film it.

Do not begin too ambitiously with the professional rolling title unit—a frame with a motorized top roller and a friction-loaded lower roller, with the title on a roll that goes from one to the other. Usually there is a variable speed motor, so that the operator can start the movement gradually and slow it down again near the end, thus avoiding an abrupt start and stop.

If, for your own travelling titles, you decide to operate the movement by hand, you can easily control the smooth starting and stopping, especially if you rehearse it once or twice before the actual shooting. Remember that as you cannot be looking into the camera viewfinder as you operate the movement, you should arrange a sort of guide-frame just outside the field of view of the camera but accurately centred, as a guide to the end position of the title. You can, of course, line up the starting position in the viewfinder before shooting.

Horizontal title set-up

If you do not have a properly made roller unit, you may find it best to use flat card instead of rolls of title background paper. A typical card could be 12 in (30 cm) wide for our example of a photographed area 8×6 in (20×15 cm). It can be as long as needed, possibly around 30 in (0.75 m).

The simplest way to film a travelling title is to lay it on the floor between guides which you will have to rig up. You then film the title with the camera pointing vertically downwards.

A suitable guide frame can be constructed by fitting side-guide strips and retaining strips over them. The side guides will be spaced apart slightly wider than the title card width (say $12\frac{1}{8}$ in apart for title cards which are exactly 12 in wide), while the retaining strips will overlap the edges of the card slightly to prevent the card jumping up out of the guides as it is moved along. Two cross slats can be added, just outside the field of view of the lens, as a guide for the person moving the card to see when it has reached the final position.

For most amateurs, moving the title by hand through the frame will be perfectly satisfactory. Nevertheless, it is often desirable to automate the movement, and this can be done by rigging up a motorized 'pulling' device. You need to pull the card at a rate of between $\frac{1}{2}$ in and 1 in per second. Various makeshift arrangements are possible. A projector might at first sight be thought suitable, with a length of waste film attached to the title card, pulled towards the projector by threading it into the machine in the normal way. This, however, will be much too fast, since the normal projection speed of Super 8 will pull the film at 3 in per sec.

If your projector has an interchangeable sprocket and you are good at simple engineering, you could make up a small diameter capstan to fit on, in place of the top sprocket, and by using a capstan diameter of about $\frac{1}{4}$ in, you could wind on a length of thin twine to pull the card along.

One ingenious moviemaker fitted a capstan to the side of a film-spool, and then ran the projector with waste film to pull the reel around and hence turn the capstan and wind up the twine, pulling the card along.

Vertical title travelling

A similar arrangement of a card moving between side-guides can be used with the card vertical, of course, though in this case the guide frame unit has to be fixed to the wall or some other vertical surface. Obviously it must be high enough to permit the length of the title card to hang beneath the frame, at the start. If a mechanical device is used to move the card as you film, it will generally have to be used with a pulley device above it.

A suitable arrangement may have the title frame on a long wooden baseboard with the side-guides and retainers as already described, and a pulley at the top of the board. This can operate with a hand-wound spindle, such as a small tubular capstan fitted on a spool, and turned on an ungeared rewind head that may be clamped to a convenient table behind the camera. Obviously the operating cord must be positioned not to interfere with the field of view of the camera, and not to cast shadows from the lights used to illuminate the title. A typical arrangement for a vertically running title card is on p. 125.

Presgrip travelling title unit

An interesting vertically running title card unit was made for the *Presgrip* titler. Although no longer available their excellent plastic-moulded letters are still on sale throughout the world.

Presgrip's arrangement was essentially a pair of rubber rollers—like a slimmed-down clothes wringer—fitted to the bottom of their title frame. The handle attached to the end of one of the rollers, was turned and drove the card, placed between the rollers, upwards through the title-frame, with a smoothness that had to be seen to be believed.

HKS roll unit

It is not surprising that the elaborate HKS titler (p. 86) has a roll attachment unit; this is the type that has the title on a roll of paper that is wound on to the lower roller, then fed upwards through the title-frame and attached to the top roller which has a winding handle on its shaft. You now position the start of the title, and begin shooting and winding the title at the requisite speed through the frame.

Titles on rolls

Obviously it is impossible to use loose letters when the title is on a roll, so in this case it is usual for Letraset type lettering to be used. The usual arrangement is to begin with a long strip of the background paper, black or coloured, but preferably relatively matt-surfaced to avoid problems with shine as the roll moves through the title frame.

If you buy your sheets of background paper from one of the larger art and graphics shops, they will probably be able to cut your paper or card accurately to your required width on a guillotine.

Home-made roller unit

It is perfectly practical to build a roller unit for travelling titles. If using a basically wooden construction, the rollers may be made from 1 in (25 mm) — or smaller — dowel rod, with end 'spindles' inserted as accurately as possible in the middle of each end. The lower (feed) roller needs a simple friction hold-back spring to provide mild drag and keep the paper taut as you wind. The top roller needs a simple handle so that you can turn it smoothly and slowly.

The end 'bearings' can be in the side-pieces of the wooden frame, one side being made of two separate pieces of wood with opposing sideways U-shaped slots that together make the round bearing hole when clamped together with a screw and wing-nut.

If the roller unit is not part of a title bench, it can be clamped to a table and the camera set up opposite it, the camera being on a tripod in the usual way.

Flip-over titles

The flip-over title is a very simple effect. To make it, you need a title frame with a separate title card holder that is pivoted half-way up,

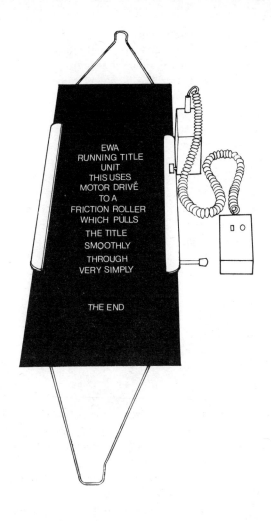

EWA
RUNNING TITLE
UNIT
THIS USES
MOTOR DRIVE
TO A
FRICTION ROLLER
WHICH PULLS
THE TITLE
SMOOTHLY
THROUGH
VERY SIMPLY

THE END

Smooth movement of a running title is most easily achieved by using a geared motor drive. This Ewa unit has guides at either side, through which the title slides, transported by a friction roller on one edge. The speed can be adjusted on the motor-control box, linked to the motor unit by a coiled connecting cable.

so that it can be rotated through 180 degrees. You now take two title cards; mount one on one side of the holder, and the other on the opposite side, upside down in relation to the first card.

It is now a simple matter to start filming with the first card in view, then at the desired moment to flip over the title holder bringing the second title into view.

Various small refinements to the actual card holder are found on some of the commercial flip-over units. These include a knob or handle on the end of the spindle for the flip-over frame, title holders that do not have a bar across the top and bottom, so that the edges of the title remain invisible as it flips over, slight friction on the swinging part, and positive stops at either end of the exact 180 degree movement.

In making a flip-over, you will normally use titles made with white letters on a black background. Two things are important. You *must* have blackness behind the title frame; a piece of black velvet is perfect. Also, you should paint the edges of the title cards black, so that these edges will not show as the title flips over. Obviously this flip-over effect is suitable for certain rather slick subjects, but it is not suitable for the transition from one title to the next within a normal film.

Zoom titles

At one time, the only way to do a zoom title was by having a titler or title bench with a long range of travel for the camera carriage along the bed. You would start the shot with the camera as far away from the title as possible, then begin shooting, moving the camera carriage along the bed towards the title card, as you were filming it. If you wanted to hold the title in focus as you went, you could do this with a suitable focusing lens by shooting single frames, altering the focus setting as well as the camera distance after each frame.

The principal virtue of the moving camera method of zooming in on a title is that you can go right up to the title card; this is quite a startling effect on the screen. This is easy to do these days with zoom lenses. If you have a long-zoom lens, say 8:1 or more, you can achieve excellent zoom-title effects. You normally

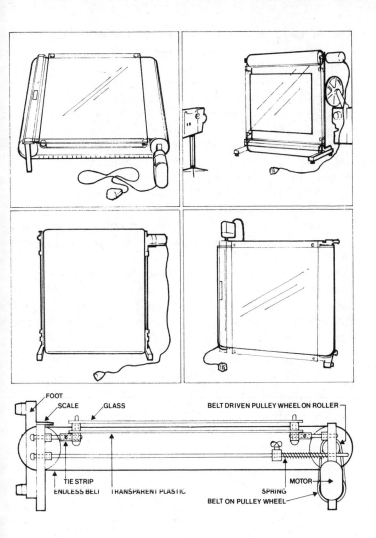

The Title-Master which uses a transparent PVC endless belt, running around two rollers. This permits titles with either moving lettering, or moving backgrounds, to be made very simply. A top glass plate and inner plastic plate allow different effects to be filmed. The unit can be stood either flat or upright for running titles, or sideways for side-to-side movements.

shoot at the minimum focusing distance (you cannot use macro on most cameras, because with most macro-focusing systems you lose the use of the zoom as such).

You must be clear, however, just *why* you want to use a zoom. It is quite a special effect, and used wrongly it can spoil the intended effect. What you must avoid is the audience being able to read the words when they are small, and continuing to read them as the words 'approach' the camera.

One example of using a zoom title is a fade-in to the title already zooming, and moving fairly quickly through the zoom and dissolving into a 'continuing' zoom-in upon the live-action scene. Remember that in practice the primary usefulness of a zoom lens on the title camera is that it lets you adjust the size of the title in the frame very easily, and allows you to see the effect in the reflex viewfinder.

Whenever you use a zoom reflex camera without looking into the viewfinder as you shoot, remember to avoid light from behind the camera going down the viewfinder tube and possibly fogging the film; some cameras have a cut-off shutter in the finder system to keep out stray light.

Superimposed Titles

Wording superimposed on a picture background is a pleasing and widely used title effect. Obviously it eases the transition between the title and the rest of the picture.

Superimposed titles lead on immediately to thoughts of the most exotic methods of double exposure in the camera, or double printing in the laboratory. There are, however, several simpler methods of achieving the same effect, even if with some loss of flexibility.

The simplest way to make titles superimposed on a picture background is with plastic-moulded (or similar) letters, laid on a still picture of suitable size. Naturally, with colour film the background picture will normally have to be in colour. And, of course, when you use a still picture as a movie background, the picture must be chosen so that its lack of movement does not appear incongruous. When you lay letters on a picture you will immediately see whether the title looks right. This is an advantage you do not have with double-exposure methods. You also have a wide choice of what you can superimpose. For example, you can use white or light-toned lettering on a dark area, or dark lettering on a light area such as the sky. With double-exposure methods, you do not have this freedom, as will be explained.

Title letters on glass

One of the simplest and most direct ways to make an in-camera superimposed title on a live-action background is to do the title wording upon a sheet of glass or other transparent material. This you support in front of the camera, which has been lined up on the background scene.

The most convenient way to do this is to hold the title glass at the end of a bracket, supported from the camera itself. A typical arrangement is to fit the title glass into the end of a fairly large type of matte box, supported in the usual way from the base of the camera so that camera and title are held firmly together, and on the film the title will look perfectly steady against the background scene. The glass holding the letters must be large enough to cover the field of view of the lens at the chosen distance.

The size of the glass will depend on the distance in front of the lens, and the focal length of the lens used. Certainly the glass should be as large as possible, in order not to have too great a difference in focus between the lettering (which will be relatively close to the lens) and the background scene which may be in the far distance.

To focus on the lettering and then to keep the background in reasonable focus, you must achieve as much depth of field as possible. Choose a relatively short focus lens, or the wide-angle end of a zoom, and work in good lighting, so that the lens can be stopped down to a fairly small aperture. If the lighting is not particularly bright, it might be desirable to use a fast film, in order to keep the lens stopped down as much as possible while at the same time ensuring correct exposure. In this way you can film the background relatively sharp, at the same time as you are perfectly focused on the lettering on the glass.

The 'glass shot' arrangement for superimposed titles is obviously an extension of the separately lit background concept which is so useful in straight titling. With the title laid out on the glass or plastic sheet, you can readily use black lettering, and superimpose it on a light area of the background—sky, for example. Alternatively you can use white lettering, which you have to illuminate from behind the camera or from the sides. Frame the shot so that the white lettering lies over a dark area of the background.

When you use white lettering lit from behind the camera, you must usually take precautions against reflections in the glass—especially from the camera itself. One method is to drape a large piece of black cloth, black velvet for example, right over the front of the camera. The lens can protrude through a small hole in the black cloth, enabling it to film the lettering on the glass and the scene behind it.

For the special superimposed title that is worth a lot of trouble, try laying out the title on a large sheet of glass using self-adhesive

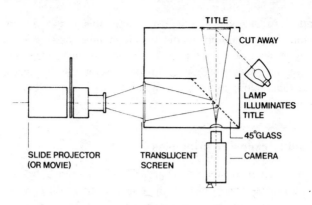

TITLE

CUT AWAY

LAMP
ILLUMINATES
TITLE

45°GLASS

SLIDE PROJECTOR
(OR MOVIE)

TRANSLUCENT
SCREEN

CAMERA

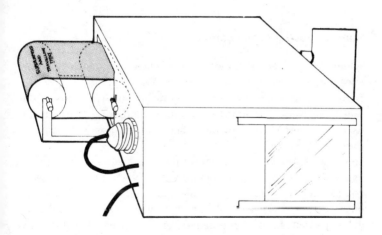

Basic arrangement of superimposing titler. The camera looks into the box
at the title card (or drum, or flap-over) via the supplementary lens, which
has a focal length equal to the title distance within the box. The title is
illuminated by a lamp. A movie or still picture is projected on a translucent
screen on the left of the box and reflected in the mirror to the camera lens.
The relative brightness of the title and projected picture may need to be
adjusted to achieve good balance.

letters, for example, and then supporting this glass in a frame upon a tripod at the appropriate distance from the camera which must, of course, also be on a tripod. The scene is then shot through the glass. To prevent reflections in the glass, it may be necessary to use black cloth to make a 'tunnel' between the camera and the glass.

Double-exposure principles

When two exposures—background picture and a title—are put on the same length of film, there are certain basic principles that control what can be superimposed on what. There are differences in procedure between shooting superimpositions in the camera and having them done afterwards in the lab. There are further differences between reversal and neg-pos, especially regarding what you can readily do with double-printing.

Superimposing in the camera

When we talk about superimposed titles, we generally mean titles made by exposing two images on the same film.

There are two ways to do this. The obvious method is to run the same film twice through the camera, rewinding in between the two exposures. Note however that rewinding is not normally possible on Super 8 cameras.

The second, less usual, method of in-camera superimposing is to use a simple optical 'trick': with a semi-silvered mirror accessory you can combine two images—title and background picture—with one single exposure. Place the semi-silvered mirror angled at 45 degrees in front of the camera lens. You can film the view through the mirror in front of the camera, and the view reflected in the mirror from the side, at one exposure. Note that the image from the side will be laterally reversed, so a reverse-lettering (mirror-image) title must be used if the title is in the side position. Remember that with a semi-silvered mirror, this will be (by definition) 50/50 transmission/reflection ratio, and this must be allowed for in calculating the exposure.

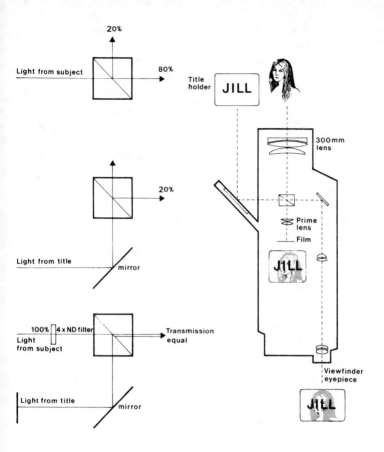

Right Schematic diagram showing the light path of the image from both the subject and the title to be superimposed. **Left** A title placed in the titleholder is superimposed automatically into the scene. By covering the lens, ultra close-ups can be made and objects only 1.2×0.85 in, will fill the frame.

Whether using double-exposure or a semi-silvered mirror accessory, you can only superimpose white (or at least light) lettering on dark areas of background. Moreover, the white lettering must be on an absolutely matt black background. This avoids all risk of surface sheen overlaying the background picture and is an important point in superimpositions. The white lettering must in effect 'burn out' the background image, otherwise you will have a ghost image showing through the lettering which would spoil the effect. Therefore, use very white lettering on a totally black background. Then you can marginally overexpose the letters, so that they will 'burn through' the background picture and remove all traces of the background picture within the letter areas.

Most superimposed titles are shot on cameras which permit *backwinding* of the film. But with Super 8 cameras the film cartridge is not designed to permit backwinding.

Backwinding Super 8

Although certainly not a recommended procedure, according to the film manufacturers, it is in fact quite possible to backwind Super 8 cartridges by using one of the special backwinder devices available commercially in Britain and Europe.

With one of these devices, take the camera into the darkroom and remove the cartridge (in the dark, to avoid fogging any of the film). Then fit the cartridge into the backwinder device and turn the handle until the required amount of film has been wound back. Now load the cartridge back into the camera, ready for the second exposure to be made on the same length of film.

One West German firm offers a device for rewinding the whole of a cartridge in which the film has been run through the camera once.

Backwinding Single-8

Unlike the commonly used Super 8 cartridge, the Fuji Single-8 cartridge is designed with the feed spool on a core that can be turned back by a spindle in the camera when you want to backwind the film. For this operation, the claw is withdrawn from the film in the gate, and then the film is pulled back by turning the core of what is normally the feed roll. This method rarely provides to-the-frame accuracy, so you may need to allow for this by shooting slightly over length and then using just the precise length you want.

Spool-loading cameras

Spool-loading cameras, 16 mm or standard 8 mm, often provide facilities for backwinding, either with a lens cap on to prevent fogging the frames during the winding back or, on more elaborate cameras, keeping the fade shutter in its fully-closed position while winding back.

Naturally you need to backwind the exact length of film to be double-exposed. The method of length-counting obviously varies between cameras. Easiest to use are ones with an actual frame counter, which is able to work both forwards and backwards. If you want to do a lot of superimposition shooting, you will be well advised to use a camera with this rather special feature. Many of the more advanced 16 mm cameras have this.

If you are using one of the older cameras with spring drive, remember *not* to wind up the spring after shooting the first scene. The backwinding itself usually winds up the spring again. And obviously if you fully wind it before backwinding, you will not then be able to backwind. Some cameras, though, have a mechanism which can be declutched from the spring motor.

Normally you should backwind one extra frame, then set the camera ready to run forward again but on the single-frame setting. When set, run one frame forward—still with the lens cap on, or the fading shutter fully-shut. The purpose of running one frame forward is to position the first frame exactly in the correct position in the gate.

Exposure for superimposition

When filming the background for a superimposed title, it should generally be slightly underexposed, rather than over. The purpose is to keep the background scene slightly dark so that the white lettering superimposed on it will show up really well.

Superimposition in the camera is the same for reversal film stock as for negative-positive. But when it comes to having super-impositions made in the laboratory, the situation is quite different.

Double printing

To superimpose white letters on a picture (or other) background by having the film double-printed—that is, run through the printer twice—it is most easily done with a reversal original, when having a reversal print made from it.

In this case, supply the laboratory with the two films. One is the reversal master of the picture background which can be moving or not, as you wish. The second film carries the lettering in clear film on a dense black background. This can be made by filming a white-on-black title card on reversal film. You can do this on ordinary reversal camera stock, normally colour, of course. Professionals sometimes use various alternatives, for example shooting on a black-and-white microfilm stock, using black letters on a white background for the original title card, and developing the film in a high-contrast black-and-white bath. In general, however, beware of using large areas of white background because it so readily tends to 'flare' on the film and cause the edges of the letters to appear less sharp than they should.

A & B roll printing

The usual method for laboratories to print superimposed titles on reversal printing—widely used in 16 mm—is by A & B roll printing. The picture film is made up into one roll and the titles are made up into a second roll, which is exactly matched for length, scene for scene. Where there are no titles to be superimposed, simply join in black leader film in the B roll, so that nothing prints from that film.

When making up the two rolls of film for A & B roll printing, you normally use a two-sprocket synchronizer and a double rewind. This way, you can supply black leader. It must be of the requisite blackness, so check first if you are unsure. When making up the rolls, remember that both should have a sufficient length of leader film on the front, with each of the two marked with a *start* frame. Normally this is marked with a large cross right across the frame, and usually with a punched hole in the centre.

When the laboratory threads the master film and the raw stock into the printing machine, they make a similar cross on the raw stock. This is used as the starting frame first for the A-roll, which is then printed and the stock rewound back to the beginning. The B-roll is then threaded, again with the start frame lined up with the start frame on the stock, and that too is printed.

Fades

When you use A & B roll reversal printing, you have the opportunity to include fades, made in the printer. In this case you simply join in the full length of the original film, continuing it right out to the end of the fade which appears in the print. Naturally the film must be carefully marked where you want fades to be made. Some laboratories offer a choice of fade length, depending on the facilities on the particular printing machine used. Join in the appropriate length of the original, and give the relevant instructions.

You can of course have fades either in or out, and you can have simultaneous fades on the title and the background picture.

Dissolves

Dissolves can also be made with A & B roll printing; for this you have a fade-out on the A-roll, superimposed on a fade-in on the B-roll (or vice-versa). Fades and dissolves on A & B roll 16mm printing are standard laboratory practice and are being used all the time—unlike optical printing of effects which is always something rather special, and usually joined into the original film for subsequent straightforward printing.

Should you want titles dissolving from one to the other, super-imposed on a background from another film, this also can be done in 16mm printing but it requires three rolls: A & B & C roll printing, for which the laboratories make an extra charge.

Negative-positive superimposition printing

As we have seen, it is simple in reversal printing to superimpose *white* lettering on a picture background by the A & B roll method. When we come to negative-positive printing, however, the situation is very different.

You can superimpose *black* lettering on to a light background by double printing of negative-positive. You could, for example, over-print black lettering into a light sky area of a background.

Mattes

To superimpose white lettering on a background picture by neg-pos printing, you have to hold back all exposure of the background in the areas you wish to appear white. Have the film with the lettering on it, black letters on clear film, and print with *both* the background film and the title film in the gate of the printer. Thus the title film *holds back* the printing in the areas of the letters. A film which acts in this way is called a *matte.*

Because of some technical problems in running three films through a contact printer which is made to run only two, matte work is usually done on an optical printer which is expensive and in general only to be used as a master for subsequent printing. It is not practical to have projection prints made wholly on the optical printer though it is normal practice to make projection prints by A & B roll 16 mm contact printing.

The optical printer is in effect a one-to-one projection printer, and a large variety of effects can be made on it. The usual practice is to join the effects film into the rest of the reel for subsequent printing of copies.

Reversal matte printing

Matte printing is also possible with reversal film but for a different situation: in this case use a matte of jet black letters on a clear background. This 'matte' film is threaded into the projector gate of the optical printer, together with the background picture

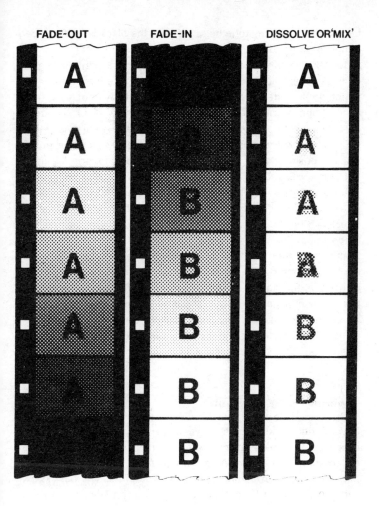

| FADE-OUT | FADE-IN | DISSOLVE OR 'MIX' |

With A and B roll printing fades in or out can be made in the printer on one or both rolls. Dissolves can be made by fading in on one roll while fading out on the other. 'Chequerboard cutting' is used when rolls are to be A and B roll printed.

film so the two films together print with the black lettering superimposed on the picture.

A further use of matte printing is for making a printing 'master' of titles which are to have coloured-body lettering and/or relief effect. A relief effect is made by making a matte by double exposure in the optical printer, displacing the camera head diagonally between the two exposures. Coloured body lettering is printed by making two mattes, one negative and the other one printed from it, positive, then using the one to hold back printing in the lettering areas and the other to fill in these clear areas with colour. There are many possibilities along these lines and all of them depend totally on the laboratory. It is true to say that almost any visual effect can be done on the optical printer as long as you are prepared to pay for it.

Remember, though, that professional services of this nature apply to 16 mm but hardly at all to the more amateur 8 mm gauges. Super 8 is the gauge more likely to offer any special facilities of the two 8 mm gauges, since standard 8 mm is now regarded as obsolete. Even so, considerable quantities of library prints are still being made in this older gauge, because of the large number of standard 8 mm projectors still being used.

Superimposing titler units

Several title-making units have been available over the years, based on the concept of a partially reflecting 45 degree mirror, to 'combine' visually *a title directly in front*—through the mirror— and *at the side, a picture reflected in the glass.* The best-known such units are the BDB Cinegraphica, and the Glanvill Lexibeam models.

Each of these consists essentially of a box, about 10 in square and about $3\frac{1}{2}$ in deep inside. There is a suitable supplementary lens built into the front window of the box, and the camera is set up so that the lens looks directly through this supplementary.

At the back of the box, directly in line with the supplementary, is the title holder. This can be a flat plate or, depending on the model, a drum for rolling titles, or a flap-over plate. The latter accessories are supported by a spindle fitting into spring-clips at either side of the back aperture of the box—the title frame, if you like.

Immediately inside the box, just behind the supplementary lens window, is the 45 degree partially reflecting mirror. This reflects from the second window in the *side* of the box, which may be a piece of ground glass or similar rear-projection screen material. So you can project a picture onto it from the outside, using either a cine or slide projector.

The only remaining essential feature is to illuminate the title, and this may be achieved very simply by placing a suitable lamp unit outside the box and shining through a special cut-out in the side of the box, and on to the title.

In the more elaborately made units, for example the Lexibeam Professional, the lamp for title illumination may be built into the box itself. In this case, suitable ventilation is provided. A further refinement is to feed this lamp through a brightness controller, either an electronic type dimmer or preferably a variable transformer. This permits easy setting of the brightness of the title in relation to the background picture. You would judge this simply by looking into the reflex viewfinder of the camera.

Although each of these titling unit boxes is complete in itself, you generally need to arrange the set-up around it of projector, camera, and if required an external lighting unit for the title.

Sometimes the components can be laid out on a large table, with packing underneath each unit to bring it to the correct height to line up with each other. An alternative arrangement is to use two adjustable projector stands for the title unit box and the projector, a firm tripod for the camera, and the lamp (if needed) on a conventional lighting stand.

Since the brightness of the projected picture on to the ground glass screen will be dependent on the projector used, you must adjust the brightness of the lighting on the title, to match up with the background picture and to give the desired 'superimposed lettering' look.

If good title lettering is used, on a really matt black background, the superimposition effect is extremely effective. It is perhaps even better with a projected slide, than movie film; the latter tends to appear unduly granular and may, with some projector and camera combinations, tend to 'strobe' slightly, giving a flickering look to the background.

As with all superimpositions, great care is needed to avoid showing any grain or greyness in the black title-card. The aim is that the white lighting from the background picture (projected on the ground glass) will largely control the level of exposure. It is therefore doubly important to match the lighting on the title, with the background picture.

Looking at a typical unit, the Cinegraphica, the supplementary lens has a power of 4 dioptres (approximately 10 in focal length). The mirror appears to be semi-silvered, with a reflection-to-transmission ratio of approximately one-to-one. The title drum or the flap-over title holder is $3\frac{1}{2}$ in wide, and the actual title width photographed should be about $2\frac{3}{4}$ in.

The ground glass is also $3\frac{1}{2}$ in wide, and the optical path distance from the supplementary lens to the title is 10 in. The distance from the supplementary, viz the 45 degree mirror, to the ground glass is 10 in. So the same width picture will be photographed on the ground glass as on the title card.

Lettering for superimposing

Lettering of the Letraset type can well be used with the super-imposing titlers, and a letter size of around 6 mm is about right for main titles, or down to perhaps 3 mm for multi-word titles such as credits. You can to some degree relate the letter size with the adjustments on the camera to include a little more, or less, of the title card, as long as you do not risk running over the edges of the title card or the projected background.

For superimposing, you will always use light (usually white) lettering on a black background. These titler units can, of course, also be used for ordinary non-superimposed titles; you may need to adjust the exposure to something different from the automatic setting on the camera, when the title is on a black background. For non-superimposed titles you can perfectly well use a coloured background if you wish.

Remember that the unit must be used in a relatively darkened room, so that no stray light will fall on the ground glass and degrade the picture on it.

Trick effects

With any of these units, various trick effects are possible. For example, you can blank out one half of the projected picture and have the title wording in the other half (as white-on-black). You could project a slide of a map onto the ground glass screen and, without adding any title, bring in a pointer as you film. You can fade in or out the lettering and/or the picture—even if only by screening off the light or closing down the projector lens with your finger. You might even do quite effective split-screen shots by using two projectors projecting on to the ground glass, with cards to mask each picture to half the width. Although colour film copied in this way does not match the fine smooth quality of the original, it is generally acceptable, especially if part of an effect that could not otherwise be achieved.

Fades and Dissolves

The most useful effect in title-making is certainly the fade. It is logical to start a film by fading in the title, and to end by fading out the end title.

When you consider the starting title in a film, it is much better for it to fade in, rather than to come on to the screen suddenly. At the end of the film, if you fade out the end title, it signifies that the film is indeed over.

A *fade-in* starts, of course, with blackness on the screen, and the image comes up gradually. The fade-in will normally take about three or four seconds to reach the normal image brightness.

The *fade-out* is the reverse, and it is made by starting from a normal image, fading to blackness, again in about three or four seconds.

A *dissolve*, sometimes called a *mix*, is simply a fade-out with a fade-in superimposed upon it. This involves making the fade-out, then backwinding the film with the lens cap on, for the length of the fade-out, and finally making the fade-in upon the same piece of film.

If you plan to do serious titling, and are thinking of buying a new camera, you should look at models with built-in fade facilities. In order to understand what you should best look for in fade facilities, it is necessary to understand a little about the various ways in which a fade can be achieved.

A fade is made by changing the exposure. For a fade-in, you will change the exposure from zero up to normal. Similarly, for a fade-out you will start with normal exposure, and smoothly reduce it to zero.

There are two basically different ways of changing the exposure to make a fade. One way is to change the *time of exposure* on each frame, by changing the shutter opening. The second way is to change the *intensity of the light* coming through the lens, by changing the lens aperture.

Variable shutter system

The most satisfactory way of doing a fade is to use a camera with a *variable shutter.* All movie cameras have a shutter, usually a sector on a rotating shaft, that cuts off the light from the film in the gate during the period of each frame cycle in which the film is being moved on to the next frame. It then opens to make the exposure when the film has come to rest. Ignoring for a moment the wide-shutter-angle XL cameras, the traditional movie camera mechanism has a shutter with an open sector of around 160 to 170 degrees.

Cameras with a variable sector shutter have a second blade on the same shaft. During normal filming, this second blade rotates together with, and behind, the main blade. However, the second blade is driven through additional gearing that, when you move a lever, varies the phasing of the second shutter with the main one. That is, it turns the second blade on the shaft and this reduces the angle of the open sector from the normal fully-open angle, right down to zero.

Almost all the cameras with a true variable shutter facility are in the upper price bracket. In some models, you operate the fade shutter by moving over a lever, smoothly, taking the usual three or four seconds to go from fully-open to fully-closed. A few cameras have the fade shutter operating via a clutch-in button, and when you press this you engage the fade shutter which is driven through the mechanism down to zero in the requisite time—an excellent system.

Some of the top models of Super 8 camera have the fade facility as part of a more or less automatic dissolve system, but you can gener-ally do a fade alone by 'abandoning' the dissolve half-way through. For a fade-in, of course, you start shooting with the shutter shut, and only open it up when it reaches its normal fully-open position and then you continue shooting the rest of the title for as long as required.

A few fade-in shutter cameras use a differently designed shutter that reciprocates up and down, instead of rotating, but the principle of the adjustable second blade is exactly the same.

The fade-shutter system has several advantages, compared with the alternative iris-fade. The shutter method is independent of lens aperture, so the time of the fade will always be the same for a constant speed of moving the lever—or of driving it automatically from the mechanism. The shutter goes positively down to fully-closed, so the picture fades completely out, as it should.

However, the fade-shutter has two fundamental disadvantages. First, it requires some rather fine instrument engineering, therefore adding to the cost of the camera. Second, and perhaps more important in practice nowadays, it cannot readily be used with true XL (existing light) cameras which have shutter-open angles of more than 180 degrees—typically 230 degrees open. But, despite these drawbacks, the fade shutter is still the best way to make fades and dissolves, and many serious users consider this factor more important than the XL facility—at least for much of their filming.

Iris fade system

The alternative system is the iris fade. Here you move the lens iris down to fully-closed, or at least as near it as possible, to make the fade-out. This works well if the camera lens has a fully-closing iris, but not so effectively if the lens iris only goes down to about *f*16 and then will move no further. To leave a faint 'ghost' image of the title completely spoils the effect of a fade-out.

For the fade-in, you start with the lens stopped down as far as possible, and start the camera running. Immediately you start to open the lens up to its working aperture, taking about three or four seconds to reach that aperture.

If you have a lens with a manually controlled iris, you can obviously manipulate it to make iris fades fairly readily, both in and out. Some automatic metering cameras include a manual override, and this can sometimes be used to make a reasonable fade, depending on how smoothly the iris can be adjusted.

Best of all, as regards making iris fades, are the automatic metering cameras that also have a built-in *electric fade* system. This simply means that the meter's moving coil, that operates the iris, is fed with increasing current at the touch of a button, and is driven from the working aperture (normally automatic) all the way down to fully-closed. The rise in current is normally arranged through a simple electronic circuit that lets the meter current build up at a predetermined rate—for the correct speed fade. The maximum current reached will correspond to the moving coil being driven right over so that the iris blades reach their fully-closed position.

This, and any iris fade system, works best when you begin at a fairly large aperture. Then the iris has several *f* stops of movement in which it can reduce the light smoothly before reaching a very small aperture and then fully-closed.

On most of these electric fade systems, you can judge the action of the iris by watching the meter needle in the viewfinder. Some fading circuits give a serious time-lag between pressing the button and the fade actually starting; with such an arrangement you should simply press the fade button that much in advance of when you wish the fade to begin.

With some cameras the drive motor stops automatically when the fade-out is complete. On other models you have to stop the camera yourself when the iris reaches the fully-closed position. Sometimes the latter is indicated by a red warning light in the viewfinder.

A fade-in is made by starting with the iris fully closed, holding the fade button pressed. Then you start the camera running and release the fade-button. The iris opens up as far as the fully-automatic setting, controlled by the metering system in the normal way. Some poorly designed iris-fade circuits give noticeable over-shoot when the iris reaches the automatic setting. It may go past this setting and then come back again to it. On the screen, this results in the picture fading in, then going past the correct exposure level and appearing too light for a moment before the iris swings back to the correct position. This effect is minimized if you can shoot at a fairly large aperture, where on most iris designs the change of aperture with a given movement is not as great as at smaller apertures.

In titling, you can generally control the amount of light on the title, and hence work at a fairly large aperture quite conveniently. You should not work completely fully open if it can be avoided, however, because focusing accuracy becomes unduly critical at very large apertures. Also, very small errors in focusing can make great differences in sharpness.

Rate of fading

What is the optimum 'law' for fading? Most professionals use a fade-shutter of the mechanically driven type, and this is used on almost all the professional optical printing machines that put in the fade in the laboratories.

The amateur normally makes fades in the camera but the principle is exactly the same. The mechanically driven fade shutter, at a rough approximation, drives the iris from fully-open to half-open in half the time of the fade. Then half of the remaining time drives a further half of what is left (that is, to a quarter open), and so on. The pattern of fading then looks like this, based on the example of a four second fade:

Start	fully open (normal exposure)
2 sec	half open (one stop less exposure)
3 sec	quarter open (two stops less exposure)
$3\frac{1}{2}$ sec	one-eighth open (three stops less exposure)
Finish	fully closed at 4 sec

Note that the exposure changes relatively slowly at first, and gets progressively faster as the fade proceeds. This seems to be a satisfactory 'law' for the fading, and a similar pattern should be used when you make an iris fade.

Speed of fade

In professional practice, different speeds of fading are sometimes used. In particular, a slower fade-out is often desirable. In any case, professionals tend to use a 4 sec fade as normal, whereas many amateur cameras seem to be rather faster.

The dissolve or mix

The widely used effect of one scene or title dissolving into the following one, is achieved by superimposing a fade-in upon a fade-out. This inevitably requires the film to be wound back in the camera for the length of the fade.

In other words, you expose the outgoing scene or title and fade out at the end of it and stop the camera at that point. Now you

148

have to wind the film back with the shutter shut or lens cap on, as appropriate, until the film is exactly at the starting point of the fade-out. Then you line up on the incoming title or scene, and start the fade-in immediately upon starting the camera.

Cameras with backwinding

With many movie cameras it is not possible to do backwinding and thus not possible to make a dissolve, even if you have a built-in fader. To make dissolves, therefore, you need a camera which permits the film to be wound back. There are several ways in which film may be wound back, and the situation is different with the various gauges.

First, Super 8—which covers the majority of movie cameras made today—is cartridge-loading. Unfortunately the ordinary Super 8 silent cartridge was not designed with backwinding in mind. There is no way to wind up the film in the feed side of the cartridge. Moreover, the take-up side has a non-return ratchet which can only be overcome with very strong pulling on the film. The sound cartridge also has no way to wind up film in the feed side once the film has been pulled out. But it does have a way in which the non-return ratchet in the take-up can be held off.

It is to the credit of the camera manufacturers that they found a way around the Super 8 problem of making a dissolve. The basic dissolve system with the Super 8 silent cartridge was first devised by G. Haufler of Bauer, during a transatlantic flight. His idea was promptly built into top-model cameras, as part of a semi-automatic dissolve mechanism.

What happens in principle is that when you want to start the dissolve, you press the button to engage its clutch which stops the take-up from turning. The film nevertheless continues to feed into the take-up chamber of the Super 8 cartridge. At the same time, the fade shutter is doing the fade-out and, when the shutter reaches fully-closed, the camera stops automatically. It is now put into reverse and a 'memory' system runs the film back for the exact length of the fade out. The film stops at the beginning of the fade-out, and is then ready to begin the fade-in.

Many of the top model cameras from various manufacturers now include the dissolving feature. The exact system varies, for example, in whether or not the camera goes into reverse automatically for the length of the fade-out, but the effect is the same: the fade-in is perfectly superimposed on the fade-out and the dissolve is technically excellent.

With this type of backwinding system, you should avoid making a dissolve when the film is more than about three-quarters used, otherwise it may jam. Certainly avoid the last few feet when you need to make a dissolve. The reason for this is that you have to feed in a 3 sec length of loose film into a nearly full take-up chamber in the cartridge and the film may not then pull out again freely when you come to wind it back.

In case of Fuji Single-8 cameras—which of course use the same film-gauge as Super 8 but a different camera cartridge shape— most of the cameras are provided with backwinding. This is easily done on Single-8 because the feed part of the cartridge has a core accessible from the outside. It only remains to fit a handle on the camera door to engage this feed core, and to retract the film-transport claw during the rewinding, and the film is readily pulled back to an unlimited degree. For the latter reason, Single-8 makes it especially simple to make superimposed titles (*see* p. 132).

For dissolves where an accurate length has to be wound back, you have to base the turns of the backwinding handle on the diameter of the film on the feed core. Most cameras have a neat gauge that tells you how many turns to wind back for a given length. With both the 16 mm and standard 8 mm gauges, the more serious cameras include backwinding, often by winding back the entire mechanism, generally one frame at a time. Since these older cameras are mostly spring drive, you should note that you must *not* wind the spring immediately before backwinding. The action of winding back the mechanism will itself wind up the spring.

Fades and wipes made with attachments

For the sake of completeness, it is interesting to remember the use of various attachments held in front of the camera lens, usually in a *matte box,* which is really not much more than an elaborately designed lens hood.

One of the less successful attachments is the *fading glass*, which is a continuously graded wedge of neutral density, from clear glass at one end to a very high density at the other. To make a fade-out, you start by shooting through the transparent end and move the wedge progressively across in front of the lens until you are shooting through the dense end of the wedge.

You should never try this with a TTL automatic metering camera because the metering will try to compensate for the density coming in front of the lens. You could, however, use it on full manual override.

The fading glass is not to be recommended because it is never sufficiently transparent and tends to fuzz-over the image immediately you start the fade. The fading glass does, however, have the virtue of being usable with even the simplest movie camera.

The matte-box, less common today than it used to be, usually has slots into which various masks or *mattes* can slide. The manufacturers generally supplied the more obvious masks such as keyhole, heart-shape, oval, and so on. Perhaps more useful was the *wipe-mask,* which simply slides across in front of the lens as the camera is running, to mask off the image gradually.

This is only really effective if done as part of a *wipe,* which requires backwinding after having 'wiped out' the outgoing scene, and ready to 'wipe in' the incoming scene. This can be very effective on titles but is difficult to achieve with manual operation of the wipe mask; the problem is to keep the outgoing wipe in exact step with the incoming wipe.

Professionally, wipes are always made in the optical printer, and a great many fascinating wipe patterns are listed by the special effects laboratories. They can wipe straight across, up, sideways, diagonally, circle-in, circle-out, star shape, heart, spiral, and many others. There are ideas here for the title maker, though perhaps the effects can be produced in other ways—by manipulating the title-cards, for example.

Iris-in and iris-out

Very popular 50 or 60 years ago, the iris-in and especially the iris-out was easily made in-camera by mounting a suitably large iris in front of the camera lens, and usually in the matte box. Do you remember Charlie Chaplin walking sadly into the distance? This was followed by a slow iris-out, which was achieved simply by closing down the special large iris unit which is far enough in front of the lens to appear reasonably sharp-edged.

To most people, this effect seems very dated and to have little potential in titling today.

Polarizing faders

The modern equivalent of the fading glass is the *polarizing fader*. This is an accessory that fits in front of the camera lens. It looks like two neutral density filters mounted together, but they are not at all. They are a very special type of filter that will *polarize* the light passing through. That is, they each act as a 'gate' that allows the light waves to vibrate only in one direction, instead of in all directions as normally.

So, by using two such filters one after the other, they will transmit the light fairly freely when their 'gates' are aligned. But by rotating one of the filters through 90 degrees, you reduce the transmission virtually to zero.

In other words, when you rotate one of the two filters through 90 degrees, you reduce the density from a pale grey to almost blackness. This is the basis of a very practical fader.

Polarizing filters have a certain density, inherently, and typically this is about the same as a 2× neutral density (ND). So when two of them are mounted together in a fader, they act like 4× ND filter (that is, they 'lose' two *f* stops of light).

This type of two-glass filter unit is mounted in front of the camera lens and you film through it while it is set at the 'light' end of its range.

To make a fade, you turn the ring or move the lever smoothly through 90 degrees in about three to four seconds. At the 'dark' end of the range, the filter will have turned almost black and this will have faded out the picture.

In practice, the dark end of the range is not fully black but usually a deep blue. This seems to be a shortcoming of most polarizing faders. It causes the picture to fade out usually to a very dark

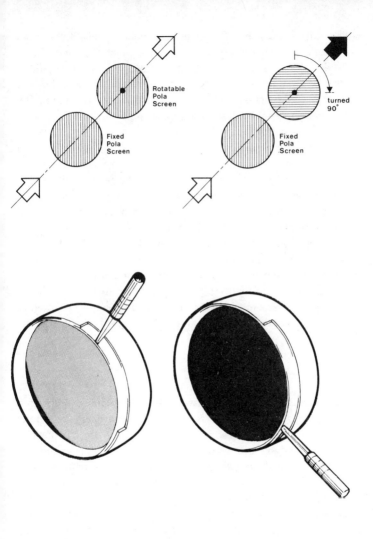

Two polarizing filters are arranged one immediately after the other. One of them is fixed; the other can be rotated through 90°. When the polarizing axes are aligned, light is transmitted through both filters, and the fader is "open". When the moveable filter is turned through 90°, the polarizing axes are in opposition and virtually no light is transmitted through. The rate of fading can be controlled by how quickly the filter is turned.

bluish image. Any bright highlights—specular reflections from water for example—will still just be visible, which is a pity.

Needless to say, when you use this variable neutral density filter, for that is what it is, on a camera with automatic through-the-lens metering, you must set the lens aperture *manually*. If not, the TTL metering system will try to compensate for the reducing light when you make the fade.

When setting the exposure, remember also to allow for the density of the filters when they are in the so-called *fully-open* position (ie: the light end of the range of the fader). With a TTL metering system, use the camera as its own meter: simply take the reading through the fader at its 'fully-open' position and then set the aperture manually at the indicated reading.

Though polarizing fader units are relatively expensive, they are a very neat way to make fades on a camera without either variable shutter or iris-fade facilities. The shortcomings obviously are that that you need more light (four times as much to reach the same aperture, on most such units), and the fade does not go down to absolute blackness if there are any really bright highlights in the subject.

Stick-on fades

A very simple way to add quite moderately effective fades to a finished film is to use *stick-on fades*, which are available from good cine dealers. Usually these fades work on the Letraset principle: they are printed in black ink on a temporary backing paper support. To apply one of these effects to a film, lay out the film on a firm surface, holding it down with adhesive tape so that the film lies flat with the emulsion side upwards. Then carefully register the effect over the film, and rub the back of the support paper with a stylus or an empty ball-point pen. Take care not to let the backing paper move until the whole length of the fade has been transferred to the film.

Fades for this method are usually printed with a half-tone dot screen pattern, so the result lacks the smoothness of a normal fade made photographically.

Various other effects such as wipes, iris-in, iris-out, and zig-zags are also made, and these in fact prove more effective than the 'half-tone dot' fades.

The wearing properties of the applied fades are usually rather poor, but it is helpful if you can apply a protective varnish over the transferred effect; Letraset *102 Letracote Gloss,* available in aerosol cans, works well.

Fades in the laboratory

For the 16 mm user who wants to make reversal prints from the camera master film (reversal original), it is a very simple matter to have fades (in or out) added during printing. So if you plan to have prints made for projection, this is acceptable way to work.

A printer fade is achieved on modern colour printing machines by fading down the printing light to zero, automatically, upon receipt of a cue (on the film) to start the fade.

Various fade lengths are obtainable on some machines and, of course, a fade-in is the reverse procedure: starting with the printing light control shutters or 'light valves' closed, and opening them up progressively until they reach the desired printing light levels for the particular scene.

When you have fades added during printing, obviously your camera master will not contain the fades. In any case, you should not project a master which is intended as an original from which to make prints.

Note that when you shoot 16 mm negative-positive—whether colour or black and white—you cannot have fades added in this simple way. So, for negative-positive titles, it is all the more important to make your fades in the camera. There is, in fact, a method that some laboratories use for fades in negative-positive prints, but this is more involved and is discussed on p. 158.

Lap dissolves in the laboratory

Reverting to 16 mm reversal prints, the laboratory can make lap dissolves quite easily, although they will charge extra for this service. The procedure is known as *A & B roll printing* and it involves making up the master into two rolls in exact frame-for-frame sync all the way through, with totally black leader-film used where printing is not required.

As the lap dissolve is simply a fade-out with a fade-in superimposed on to it, you can have the outgoing scene on the A roll, and the printer makes the fade-out. The entire roll would be run through the printer even if all the rest were black leader.

The printed film-stock is then rewound in the dark and rethreaded on the printer with the B roll. In this roll nothing will actually be printing until the fade-in starts, exactly superimposed on the fade-out that was made on the previous printing.

This is a perfectly standard laboratory practice nowadays, but remember that most laboratories have a minimum order charge; it is rarely economical to have short lengths duped, just to introduce a fade or dissolve. It pays, when shooting titles, to make your fades and dissolves in the camera if you possibly can.

Chequerboard cutting

In the event that you have to use A & B roll printing to introduce dissolves into the first scene of the picture, perhaps from the last of the main titles, it is worth considering a neat way of making the joins invisible on the print.

This also applies on 16 mm and is known as *chequerboard cutting*. The idea is to use a splicer with a one-way overlap, and to have the overlap on the black leader. Each scene is then joined on to alternate rolls. Thus the A roll will have scenes 1, 3, 5, 7 etc, and the B roll will have scenes 2, 4, 6, 8, etc.

In between scenes you splice a length of black leader, of exactly the same length as the corresponding scene on the other roll.

For making up A & B rolls, you need a two-way synchronizer and twin rewinds. When splicing for chequerboard cutting, remember that all the joins on one roll overlap one way, while all the joins on the other roll overlap the other way—that is, always overlapping onto the black leader.

Negative-positive dissolves

You can have lap dissolves made with the printer shutters, in negative-positive printing, with A & B roll printing.

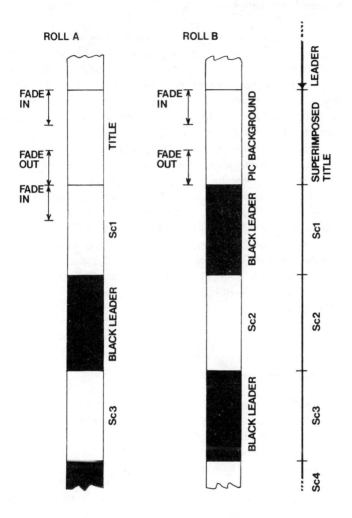

A and B roll printing with superimposed titles is standard practice with 16 mm reversal originals. Titles are assembled in the A roll and the picture assembled in exact sync in the B roll.

Negative-positive fades

Some laboratories will do negative-positive fades in 16mm A & B roll printing by the principle of *fogging out* on the print.

To do this, the scene is in the A-roll and a length of *clear* leader is in the B-roll. For the fade-out, the printer light on the B-roll comes up from nothing to full on, so progressively 'blacking out' the image printed from the A-roll. This results in an acceptable fade. It is technically possible to do the same thing without the complication of A & B roll printing, simply by running the raw-stock through the printer without any negative, and controlling the printer light to make the fogging-out fades at the appropriate times in the film. In practice, this can only be achieved with counters whose fade-cueing is independent of the negative film as, for example, on printers with what is known as *frame-count cueing*. This uses an electronic counter that counts the frames starting from the first sync mark, and cues in the fades electronically on the chosen frames. Most of the printers in use in the laboratories do not have this type of cueing, but in fact depend on cues added to the edge of the film.

Super 8 laboratory work

Super 8—and indeed standard 8mm—gives excellent quality when you project the camera original. But prints—duplicates or 'dupes'—are almost invariably disappointing.

The truth is, of course, that the small-format film just does not have enough reserve of quality to stand duplicating with impunity, at least with current materials and laboratory techniques. So Super 8 work is not done by most laboratories in the same way that they all do 16mm. Indeed, virtually all Super 8 printing is from larger gauge originals, though a contact intermediate negative is often made from which the final prints are produced.

There is very little specialized laboratory work on Super 8, and for that reason also it is important to do virtually all fades, lap dissolves and superimpositions in the camera.

Fades by chemical treatment

For the sake of completeness, we must remember two 'chemical' methods of making fades. Both are messy and not much used nowadays, since fades are so much more easily made in the camera, if you have the right sort.

The first method is *dye fades,* applicable to reversal film or positive print. Here the film is made to take up a controlled amount of strong neutral density (ie: black) dye solution, by varying the time of immersion—the dark end of the fade being immersed in the solution for the longest time.

The second method is only applicable to black and white negative film, and this is to use a silver bleach solution to bleach away a controlled amount of the silver image—again by controlling the immersion time. When the image has to be completely faded out, the entire silver image is bleached away at the end of the fade, and hardly bleached at all at the other end.

Dye fades

To make a dye fade, pour the dye solution into a long narrow tube—a deep test-tube, for example.

Now take the film in which you wish to make the fade, with the end to be faded out lying at the outside end of the length of film. Feed the end of the film into the dye solution, one frame at a time, taking about 5 sec per frame—depending on the dye solution. The longer the film is in the dye, the more dye it will absorb, and the darker that piece of film becomes.

When the required length of film has been immersed—the final few frames hardly having much time at all in the dye—the film is quickly withdrawn, rinsed under a tap to remove the surplus dye, and blotted off.

To make sure that the last few frames of the fade reach as good a black as possible, these last few frames are inserted in the dye solution again and left for about 5 min to soak up the maximum amount of dye. The film is finally withdrawn, rinsed and blotted off again on a paper towel or tissue, and hung up to dry.

If you have a well formulated solution, the dye fade method works fairly well, but there is always the problem that dye solution strong enough to give a reasonable black will tend to over-dye the start of the fade-out. The optimum dye strength is, therefore, a compromise—unless you care to go to the trouble of having two different dye strengths.

One of the most effective dye-fade solutions ever made was Johnsons *Cine Fade*—now, sadly, no longer being made.

A formula published many years ago used a mixture of dyes to give reasonable neutrality, though the exact quantity of each dye may need adjustment, according to the particular samples of the dyes used.

Dye-fade solution

Anthracene Acid Brown B	9 gm
Methylene blue	9 gm
Napthol green	9 gm
Water	1000 ml

The mixture should be filtered before use.

The problem with mixing your own solution is the very practical one of obtaining the dyes. Today, if you want to buy a few kilos of dye, there is no problem. But nobody wants to sell just a few grams.

Whether the mixture of coloured dyes is the best approach, or whether it is better to use a near-neutral colour dye as a basis, is a matter for experiment. Dyes such as *Nigrosene Black* spring to mind as obvious possibilities.

For the experimenter, a highly practical and inexpensive way to procure dyes is to use household dye mixed at great strength—something between 1 per cent and 5 per cent is generally possible. The household 'cold water dyes' are usually suitable, such as *Dylon Cold Water Dye,* in the black shade.

You can experiment with dye strengths and dyeing times, and with the particular type of film you wish to treat. The problem is to make the relatively thin gelatin emulsion layer take up sufficient dye to achieve a good black at the end of the fade-out.

Modern emulsions are relatively hard, too, and they do not want to take the dye evenly, especially if greasy. In the latter case,

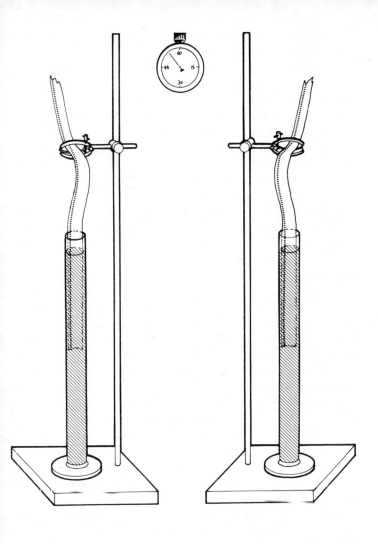

Feeding film into a cylinder, a couple of frames at a time, for a controlled amount of time. The film is fed into dye for a dye-fade and into reducer for a chemical fade (for black and white negatives).

clean the film with one of the film-cleaner solvents, for example Freon 22, or methyl chloroform (1:1:1-trichloroethane). Do not confuse the latter with trichlorethylene, which is a very different thing. Incidentally the trichloroethane is fairly safe with striped film. In the old days you would probably have used carbon tetrachloride (CTC) as a film-cleaner, but this is no longer acceptable because it is known to be toxic.

The length of film to be dyed for a fade is generally about 3 sec of screen time, and this is 9 in (about 23 cm) on Super 8 which runs at 18 fps, for example. Super 8 at this frame speed runs at exactly 3 in-per-second, in fact.

The 16 mm length, normally with 24 fps speed, is much more unwieldy, and the necessary 72 frames occupies just under 2 ft (22 in or 55 cm).

Bleach fades

On black and white negative film, you can make a fade by bleaching out the negative image to a controlled degree per frame. Thus, at the end of the fade-out the silver image is bleached away completely, so that it prints black when printed.

The negative silver image is bleached by immersing it in Farmer's Reducer, a frame at a time, until at the end the image is bleached away to nothing, and progressively reaches this from the normal image at the start of the fade-out. You can adjust the dilution of the mixed reducer to achieve a reasonable bleaching time. In practice you are likely to use only 16 mm in black and white negative form, and here a 3 sec fade represents 72 frames (at 24 fps).

A typical formula is to use a stock solution of 10 per cent potassium ferricyanide (poison), and to mix this *just before use* with plain hypo solution (not acid). For the 10 per cent solution, dissolve 10 gm of the potassium ferricyanide in about 70 ml of water and make it up to 100 ml when all dissolved.

To mix the fade solution, a good starting point is to add 10 ml of the ferricyanide solution to 100 ml of 20 per cent plain hypo solution (*not* acid hypo), and start lowering the film into this, a frame at a time.

Typically, the film will want a maximum bleaching time of around

2–3 min to bleach the silver image right away at the one end of the fade, and only a few seconds at the minimum-time end, that is, the beginning of the fade-out.

It is useful to wet the film first, to assist even penetration by the reducer. The film must be thoroughly washed afterwards to remove virtually all the hypo solution, just as any negative film needs to be washed well after developing and fixing. 10 min in running water is suitable, as long as the water has good access to the film all over — do not simply leave the film lying in a coil. After washing, wipe off surplus water and, in particular, remove all droplets from the back of the film, then hang it up to dry. If the film has not yet been edited — and it is best to do chemical treatment *before* editing — it is convenient to wet the entire scene to avoid drying marks due to wetting only part of the film.

This bleaching method of making a fade on negative film works well if you take care and the conditions are right. But it is *not* suitable for colour film.

In any case, on titles it is better and easier to make your fades in the camera.

Special Inserts

Titling often involves shooting material other than actual titles. The whole point of movies is to show things visually. Often you can achieve this by filming special inserts such as maps, sections from postcards, guide books, programmes, and so on.

Copyright

But first a warning about copyright. Though the law differs from country to country, the basic principle holds that copyright exists in pictures etc, just as in the written word (and also music). Thus you cannot legally rephotograph pictures without written permission from the owner of the copyright. This may involve paying a fee.

To return to the matter of shooting special *inserts,* as they are known professionally, close-up shots of this nature are generally made on the title bench, or at least with the same sort of set-up as you would use for titling. *Titles and inserts* are the shots that involve close-up filming, to be cut into the rest of the film.

Close-up filming

Most inserts are of flat copy, and generally the original material will be only a matter of inches wide. So close-up filming is quite usual for inserts, just as for much title-making.

Exactly the same close-up arrangements apply, and the reflex viewfinder type camera will almost invariably be used, because it makes the lining up so easy. You may need to make a viewfinder test (*see* p. 62), if the subject calls for accurate lining up.

If your zoom lens, at its nearest focusing distance and full tele-photo setting, will not go down to a sufficiently small photographed area for what you have to film, you can usually add a supplementary lens to enable you to move the camera closer (*see* p. 26). Alternatively, many zoom lenses today include a *macro* setting for filming at closer distances. This makes use of the zooming components of the lens which are switched to a special close-up focusing mode. Very careful focusing is important when the camera is used in the macro mode.

As regards viewfinding, remember that most amateur movie cameras include more in the picture than you see in the finder. You are strongly recommended to make a test, to check exactly what your particular camera actually does include. If you have not yet done this, then play safe and keep *well* within the edges of your subject. Otherwise you will probably find you have included the edges of the original in the picture on the screen. This looks very shoddy and you should invariably retake the shot without the edge being in-picture. Always try to maintain the highest technical standards in your titles and inserts.

Lighting for inserts

Flat copy is generally not very critical as regards lighting. If the light is even, and as long as nothing reflects from the surface into the camera lens, all will be well. You can easily use the basic 'two lamps at 45 degrees' layout that is used for much titling. As many inserts are of relatively small originals, one lamp alone may well be adequate.

Three-dimensional subjects need more careful lighting because the aim is to simulate natural lighting. This may mean having a definite *key light* as the main source, a *fill-light* to light up the shadows to a natural degree, and a certain amount of *back-light* to lift the subject out from the background. And just like a full-scale subject, you may need separate lighting on the background, if this is much separated from the subject. All this is standard lighting practice—in miniature!

You must, however, remember *continuity*. If your insert is a close-up shot of something in the film that has just been seen in a full-size scene—a hand in close-up writing a letter, for example—the insert must match the full-scale shot in all respects: lighting, hand, type of pen, size of paper, background, and so on. As the insert is in close-up on the screen, any wrong details are instantly noticeable. For this reason, it is generally best to shoot such inserts *after* you have shot the full-scale scene, and preferably when you already have the processed film for reference.

Movement on 'stills'

The basic concept of movies is that you are taking pictures of *moving* subjects. So when filming inserts of still subjects—whether pictures or of actual subjects—it is often desirable to add movement to the shot. In this way you avoid giving the impression of a static shot cut into a movie.

You can add movement—but very *slowly*—either by using the zoom or by tracking across the subject either horizontally or vertically: such movement *must* be very slow. Properly done, you will find this remarkably effective in hiding the fact that you are taking still subjects. The slight movement—perhaps not even on every shot—seems to avoid admirably the 'lantern slide' look.

Some years ago a company in New York made a 12 minute film about the Cibachrome colour printing process. Except for one live-action sequence in the middle showing the processing procedure, the whole of the film was made from stills. Pictures from the history of colour printing, pictures showing the use of colour, slides of photo-dealers whose voices were overlaid on the track from tapes, all were filmed on the animation bench. Full use was made of the movements, so that the pictures were hardly still on the screen for a moment. The film zoomed in slowly, imperceptibly, tracked across, cut, cut on fast shots, faded, dissolved, used overlaid sound to take attention from the stillness of still pictures, and all this done so skilfully that no lay audience would realize it was a film largely made up of still pictures and colour slides.

Sound for Your Titles

Today, everyone expects films to have sound, just as they expect sound with television. And, obviously, you need sound on the titles as well as on the film itself. Even if the film is live-sound throughout, the titles still need sound, generally music, added.

If you shoot the titles on a live-sound camera, you still almost invariably add the sound *afterwards,* on the projector. So there are two basic situations for sound on titles. First, the film where only the titles need sound added, because the rest of the film already has sound on it. Second, where sound is to be added to the whole film.

Adding sound to titles only

Before you start shooting titles to which music is to be added, plan the exact lengths of the titles in relation to the music you are using with them. Never shoot the titles without knowing exactly what the music will be like for length.

Assume that you have chosen the music for a particular introductory title or sequence of titles. Study the length of the music in relation to the proposed length of the titles by timing the music with a stop-watch. Check the number of seconds from the start to the closing bars of the music you wish to use.

It is usually satisfactory to start the title with a fairly quick fade-in (if your camera has a fading facility). You must check whether the length of the music is reasonable in relation to the title. You do not want to have to hold a two-word title through 20 seconds of music; this would be incongruous. You could use a shorter piece of music, or rewrite the title—perhaps adding a second one after it—to bring it up to a reasonable length to match the music. At the end of the title it is an excellent idea to fade out the picture (if your camera has this facility), particularly if you are also fading out the sound.

Titles for live-sound films

If your opening shot following the title is live-sound, remember that when you cut the title onto this, the sound on the incoming scene will not start, on Super 8, until 18 frames (2 sec at 18 fps) after the join, when you are projecting. This is the standardized separation between picture and sound on Super 8. A fade-out of the music at the end of the title helps to make an easy transition into the (slightly late) sound on the incoming scene.

When recording tracks on title material that is going to be cut into live-sound film, it is safest to record the tracks separately *before* cutting the titles into the rest of the film. This procedure avoids all risk of inadvertently stopping at the wrong point, and of erasing the start of the irreplaceable live soundtrack.

Always try to shoot titles to the desired lengths, in sequence, so that you do not have unnecessary joins in your final projection copy. It is much better also if you have a length of film with no joins on which to record the track.

There is a lot to be said for shooting titles on prestriped film, either on a sound camera or using one of the prestriped films now available in silent cartridges. In this way, you avoid the need for sending the film away to be striped after processing.

Sound levels

When adding sound on the projector, it is important to record the title music at a volume level that will match the live sound on the rest of the film. If your projector has a manual control of recording level, use it to set the recording level of the title music, so that it replays at a volume level matching the rest of the film.

The end title music

It is absolutely vital that your end title should exactly match the timing of the music. Nothing is more obviously amateur than the

168

music finishing when the picture still has some way to go. Almost as bad is the end title music not playing until the title has already come and gone.

When you add music to the titles only—before cutting them into the film—it is fairly easy to keep it in step with the picture. This is especially true if you dub the music on to the titles, one at a time, or a sequence at a time such as an end title followed by a credit title, or cast list, or even a traditional credit to the maker of the film: *A John Doakes Film,* or *Filmed by Joe Bloggs,* etc. In any case, the music should end with the last of these titles. On most projectors, for sound fades you can use the so-called trick or superimposition knob to produce fades of the music.

One of the fundamental advantages of magnetic stripe recording is that if the recording is not right the first time, you can do it over again on the same length of film. You will of course automatically erase the earlier track as you record the replacement one. Do not be satisfied until you have the track as correct as you can make it.

Adding sound all through

If you have a silent film which has been striped you may wish to join on the titles, front and back, and then record the entire track through both the titles and the rest of the film. Depending on the complexity of the track, your equipment and your ability as a sound mixer, you can either record the whole track right through, bringing in new sound sources as necessary, or in some cases you can record one section at a time using the superimposition control on the projector to bring in each new section of sound without introducing clicks.

The more professional users will normally prefer to dub the entire track right through. If need be, a small team of people can be assembled to operate the various pieces of equipment, on cue. For example, the title music may be on a record and, at the end of this, the following music might be on tape. If you have two or more sound sources, you may need a mixer unit with the requisite number of inputs, to enable you to control and mix, or bring up on cue, the respective signal sources. A few of the more elaborate projectors include mixing facilities for two or more inputs, so these models may not need an external mixer. Most films have some or all of the sound added afterwards, and only rarely at the time of shooting. This is usually because there was little or no interesting sound at the time of shooting, or sometimes a lot of sound, all of which was unwanted!

Recording music plus commentary

Films such as travelogues and holiday movies generally have background music with commentary. This can sometimes be done on the run. It is usually easier, however, to record the music all through and then to rewind the film and go through it again, recording the speech in the appropriate sections by using the superimposition feature which is on most good sound projectors. You can either cue by stop-watch (assuming that your projector is always at the same speed setting) or by a counter on the projector. Many of the better sound projectors now have a built-in counter for cueing.

Choosing the simplest procedure

There are many ways of working when recording tracks. For example, the whole track can be recorded on tape which is then transferred to the striped film. Multitrack operation can be used on the tape; for example, if you record the two tracks one at a time, you can save a lot of panic in adhering to cues. You then play off the two tracks together when transferring the tape track on to the striped film.

It is now generally accepted that the film you project should have the soundtrack actually on it. The days of projecting with tape synchronizers are happily ending. The universal feeling today is that the sound should be on the film itself, on the magnetic stripe. But you can, of course, use all the tape synchronizing gear you wish for transferring from tape to stripe when making the film and when 'assembling' the track.

Sound on stripe

With conventional magnetic recording, you record on to the magnetic stripe on the film. Even if you are not going to do live-sound shooting, and in title-making you hardly ever record the sound at the same time, there are definite advantages in shooting on *prestriped* film (that is, sound-type movie film). To do this you normally need a sound camera, which you can easily use in its silent mode. You then add the sound to the track later.

If you shoot on silent (unstriped) film, you can send the film away after processing, to a company that will put on the stripe for you. Some people do home-striping successfully, but as a procedure it has several variables that are not easily kept under control by the casual user. Indeed, results of home-striping can be disastrous: either the stripe goes on in the wrong place or peels off again later. Worst of all, badly put on stripe causes differential shrinkage in the striped area. This renders the film quite unusable and takes some years to become apparent.

The safest way is to use factory-striped stock or to have the film subsequently coated with a paste stripe. Of the two, the factory-striped stock generally has the smoothest stripe because of its smoother surface; being striped in no-join rolls, the stripe coating can be pressure-rollered flatter and smoother. In contrast to this, amateur striping services doing coated stripe often have to cope with edited (joined) films, which cannot have the same 'brute force' calendering applied after coating, thus leaving a rougher and less flat surface.

Where to find title music

There are three basic sources of music for adding to titles:
(a)   special records of movie music for the amateur.
(b)   professional records specially made for film use.
(c)   commercial records.
Each has advantages and disadvantages that should be considered.
(a) For many users, special records offered for amateur moviemakers are the best way of providing title and background music. These

records are offered only by a few specialized firms, and generally contain a good selection of different 'moods' of music.

They have the great advantage of being made for amateurs to dub (that is, to use for re-recording) without any further royalty payments beyond the initial cost of the disc or tape. Against this convenience is the obviously limited selection of such records, and hence of the types of music available.

(b) Special discs (and tapes) offered for dubbing are designed primarily for the professional film industry, and a huge selection is available from the few specialist firms in this business.

Their catalogues list hundreds of records for all moods and situations. Among the listings one finds special records with bands of title music of various short lengths. Often there is starting, bridging and end-title music in matching styles, recorded in separate sections, each one self-contained.

You should certainly procure the catalogues of the 'mood music' discs and tapes available from the specialist firms; they are well worth the small charge made for them, for they give brief descriptions of the music and the timing of each piece. The method of charging for using this music varies from firm to firm. A widely used procedure is to make a charge for the record itself, then to charge a dubbing fee when you use the music in a film. This includes copyright clearance.

(c) The ordinary moviemaker naturally thinks first of using commercial records as a source of music for transferring on to movie sound tracks. But there is a problem: *copyright*.

The law varies in different countries, but the same basic principles apply. The situation is perhaps most efficiently organized in Britain and rather less so in the USA.

In Britain there are three distinct copyrights. First, the composer holds copyright in his composition, and this lasts until 50 years after his death. Second, the performers playing the music hold copyright in their actual performance on the record. Third, the record company holds copyright in their recording.

Solving copyright problems

Before you can legally dub (that is, re-record) from a record, even for private purposes, you have to obtain *copyright clearance*. This normally involves paying fees. The same thing applies to certain other situations such as public performances. If, for example, you run shows in a hall to which the public are admitted, the hall has to be licensced for the playing of records. And every individual record must be listed and paid for.

In Britain an admirable scheme of licensing has been negotiated for amateur moviemakers by the IAC (Institute of Amateur Cinematographers), and there does not seem to be any similar scheme operating elsewhere in the world. Briefly, this involves the payment of very modest sums of money for three licences, as follows:

1 A licence to record copyright music. This is issued on behalf of the Mechanical-Copyright Protection Society Limited which controls more than 90 per cent of music in general use. All such licences are strictly for amateur use only.

2 A licence to copy discs and tapes bought in shops and stores. This is issued on behalf of the British Phonographic Industry. It waives the prohibition on copying such recordings, provided the sound tracks made in this way are strictly for amateur use. Furthermore, the musical works must comprise only orchestral, bands or choruses. Note that recordings of solo performers are normally barred, as collective arrangements are impossible. This licence does *not* cover the special mood music records from the specialist firm such as Boosey and Hawkes, because those recordings are cleared automatically by the MCPS licence in **1** above.

3 A licence to reproduce in public, music dubbed from discs, or tapes bought retail. This is issued on behalf of Phonographic Performance Limited, who control public performances of recordings made by the British record companies.

We are indebted to the IAC (63 Woodfield Avenue, Ashtead, Surrey, England) for permission to quote from their information, and full details will be supplied on request directly to them. The operation of this scheme is one of their most valuable services to members, but it should be noted that it only applies to Britain and not to other countries.

Home-made music

The simplest way to avoid all music-copyright problems in your films is to find someone who will compose your music specially.

Some highly successful amateur films have used specially composed music played by a local amateur group of musicians—some of whom certainly approach professional standards.

True, this means doing your own recording. When a film is a club effort, there is usually someone within call with reasonable expertise in music recording who will help in putting the music on to a master tape. From this, it can be dubbed on to the final magnetic stripe sound track on the film.

Several prizewinning films have been made with solo guitar, using expertly improvised music that exactly suits the mood of the film. There are other obvious possibilities: piano, for example, or electric organ.

Choosing title music

The title music must be chosen to set the mood for the film which follows. The music immediately becomes an integral part of the film, which would be less effective without it. Hence the name *mood music* which is generally used for records specially made for dubbing. A glance at the index of a mood music catalogue, under the heading of *Titles, Links, and Ends,* reveals an almost unbelievable choice.

When choosing title music, there are two ways of working. You might want a passage of music the exact length of the titles, or more likely you have to shoot the titles to match the length of the music. You would use this sort of title music when your film itself has live sound on it, right from the start.

The second choice of title music is the sort that deliberately runs on into the film, when it becomes the background music. This kind of title music is used, for example, on the track of a scenic film, or a documentary which is to have a music plus commentary track. Here you may try and find a piece of music that has a definite change of pattern at the end of the titles. Sometimes, however, you can achieve a similar effect with a deliberate change in volume level at the end of the titles. To make this a smooth transition, you should make the titles of the right length to finish at a suitable point in the music, at which it would be logical to expect a change in volume level.

Always consider the titles and the music together, particularly as regards the length. In the case of end titles, it is often helpful to consider the timing from the *end* of the music. In this way, you can work the timing backwards from the end, and thus ensure that the title and the music end together.

Cartooning

Filming your own cartoons is very much akin to titling. Indeed, the professionals use exactly the same sort of animation stand or 'rostrum' for filming titles as they use for cartoons. To make your own cartoon film—even a short, simple and relatively crude one— is one of the most rewarding tasks in movies. For the creation not just of the characters, even simple 'stick men', but of making them *move,* is entirely up to you; it epitomizes the whole-world of movie-making, in a way that no ordinary filming can do.

Cartooning depends on *persistence of vision,* as indeed does the art of movies itself. The human eye retains the image it has just seen for a fraction of a second. So when you show a number of slightly different pictures in quick succession, the eye will see them as one continuous picture. If each individual picture is made slightly different, the eye will see the differences as movement. This is the basis of animation in cartooning—and of stop-action titling (*see* p. 115). To do your own cartooning, you make a succession of drawings, normally one for each frame of film to be exposed.

If you make a film to run at the normal Super 8 speed of 18fps, you will need 18 drawings for every second of screen-time. To draw a character raising his arm in a time of one second, you divide the movement into 18 discrete steps on successive drawings.

You then film the drawings in succession, using the single-frame release to expose one frame of film at a time. When the processed film is projected, the character is seen to raise his arm smoothly— an effect which is intriguing the first time you do it and which scarcely loses its fascination even after years of experience.

Making a start

To a large degree, your success in making a cartoon film depends on your artistic ability. Yet even if your skill is minimal, there are several shortcuts you can take.

You can start very effectively by drawing simple 'stick men'. Or you can use tricks like having a drawn character with a pivoted arm which is cut out and laid on the main drawing. Then only the arm is moved in a succession of frames. You can trace from and adapt an already drawn basic character, altering small details like the position of arms and legs, shape of mouth to produce a smile, and so on.

Many professionally made examples of cartoon films—TV commercials, for example—use incredibly simple characters. If you study them, you can see they are quite within your own capabilities as long as you are prepared to sit quietly and 'have a go'. Try doodling on a blotter or a scrap pad. Draw a round face with two large round dots for eyes and two small dots for a nose. Now try various shapes of mouth to change the expression (*see* p. 179).

Successive drawings

The basis of cartooning is that each drawing leads on from the last one. To achieve this, you need to have each new drawing *registered* with the one before. A simple and effective (though crude) way to do this is to locate each sheet into the corner of an L-shaped piece—rather like printing bromide paper enlargements in the darkroom, and putting the paper into the corner of the masking frame to locate it. In fact, you could even use a masking frame to hold the drawings when making them, and then again when filming them.

Pin bars

Professional cartoon makers always punch holes along the edge of each blank sheet of paper or cel, before doing any drawing on it. Then each sheet is fitted on to a *register pin bar* during drawing, and then later for the filming operation, thus keeping each new frame in exact register with the ones before and after it. The simplest register punch you could use would be the ordinary office punch, as used for loose-leaf filing. A typical one has holes on 80 mm centres. That is, the distance between the centres of the holes is exactly 80 mm. You can make pin bars, preferably of metal, but even wood has been put to good use by enthusiastic amateurs. Always make or obtain pin bars in pairs—one for drawing and the other for filming. Then you do not have to transfer just one pin bar from one job to the other.

Various pin bars are available on the market. Oxberry use two $\frac{1}{4}$ in diameter pegs on 8 in centres. They also make an excellent punch for this gauge of pin bar, though it is rather expensive for the beginning amateur and is aimed mainly at the media studios.

Kodak make register pin bars and punches for their graphic arts register system. These use the excellent and very professional principle of one hole that fits its pin accurately, while the other hole allows for shrinkage sideways by providing sideways clearance (*see* p. 181).

Professional cartoon benches such as Oxberry and Disney use further elaborations of the one register hole for location and one or more slots which prevent slewing. The punches for these professional standards are invariably very solidly engineered and correspondingly high in cost.

Filming

The whole basis of cartoon film making is to take the pictures one frame at a time. So you need a camera that lets you give single-frame exposures. Furthermore, the camera should let you make the single-frame exposures *easily,* without fuss or strain or undue moving around and in particular without risk of moving the camera at all. Some cameras, especially the older models with purely mechanical drive, need such a hard push on the release trigger that you are likely to move the camera with every frame you expose. This is particularly true if your camera support is not absolutely rock-solid. Any risk of camera movement is quite unacceptable for single-frame cartoon filming.

Some cameras permit a cable release to be used which is helpful in preventing movement of the camera body when exposing each frame. Further, a sensibly long cable release can bring the releasing end to a convenient position alongside the artwork. Naturally you must make sure it does not get into the picture. Nothing is more annoying than having to get up and reach over to the camera for every frame you have to expose. So remote releasing is desirable, if not essential, for any serious amount of animation filming.

Best of all is a camera with not only electric drive but *electromagnetic releasing* as well. With this type of camera, releasing is done by a push on a press-button or a microswitch and this can be located anywhere handy near the artwork, such as by the edge of the animation table or copyboard.

With this solenoid releasing, each press of the button will expose one frame of film in the camera—assuming the controls are set for single-frame releasing. This system naturally stops the mechanism with the shutter *shut* at the end of each frame's exposure.

The simpler and frequently encountered electrical remote control system of fitting a switch circuit with the camera's motor, does *not* automatically stop the camera with the shutter shut. It is, therefore, definitely not suitable for single-frame remote releasing.

You must be sure to have *true* electromagnetic releasing. This works by a built-in solenoid (sometimes part of a relay whose contacts are doing the switching) that is energized by closing the remote switch or press-button. In turn, the solenoid does the actual releasing in the camera. When the single-frame exposure cycle has started, it continues through until the camera stops, whether or not you are still pressing the release button.

The camera will stop at the end of the one-frame cycle, and you must let go of the button and press again to expose the next frame; and so on.

If you plan to do much single-frame shooting, you will certainly find it worthwhile to use a camera with electromagnetic releasing.

The camera rostrum

The titling bench used for filming cartoon material is traditionally known as a *rostrum*. We speak of filming on a *rostrum camera,* which normally refers to the whole outfit and not just to the camera itself.

Rostrum cameras almost always work with the camera pointing down vertically, so the drawings can be laid flat on a table-top which lies horizontally, beneath the camera lens (*see* p. 199).

The table-top can be fitted with the pin or peg bar on which the cels or drawings are registered one after another as filming proceeds. Lights set at the sides shine down at 45 degrees or so to the centre of the photographed area.

From this simple concept, which is no more than a vertical titler, you can add varying degrees of complexity, depending on what you wish to do.

Platen

For a start, you will need a glass *platen* to hold the drawing perfectly flat while it is being photographed. This can be a sheet of selected white plate glass about $\frac{1}{4}$ in (6 mm) thick, laid on the drawing. If a lot of work is envisaged a more elaborate arrangement is to mount the glass on a skeleton frame, hinged at the back so that you simply lift up the front to raise the platen for changing the drawings.

It is important that the glass should be *self-aligning,* to lie perfectly flat on the artwork, and not be constrained by the frame around it. It is usual to support the glass along its centre-line from side-to-side by mounting it from a swivelling holder at each side of the frame. Stops should be added so that the glass remains approximately in line with the frame when the platen is raised. Professional platens often add a spring toggle action on the hinge of the frame that carries the glass. The toggle ensures that when raised, the frame will remain up automatically, so that you have both hands free when changing the drawings.

Camera orientation

You will normally make your drawings on paper or cels with the register holes punched along the *top*. This way, you avoid having the register under your hands when doing the drawing. It is best to have the artwork *the right way up* on the rostrum when seen from your working position at the front. You *must* have the camera the same way up as the artwork. The camera support on the rostrum must be designed accordingly. As the base of the artwork is towards

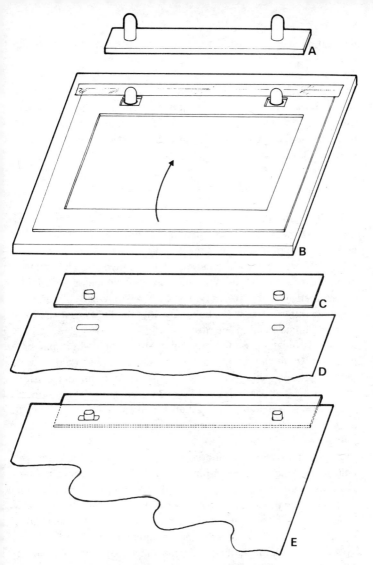

A Home-made wooden pin bar. **B** Wooden baseboard with holes for pins to protrude through. Cel or paper is fixed on the pins in register and a platen of cardboard or ply placed on top. This can be raised by means of a hinge made of adhesive cloth tape. **C** Kodak register pin bar (stainless steel). **D** Kodak register punch makes one hole which fits the pin exactly and a second which is longer. **E** When the punched cel is fitted to the pin bar, the righthand hole gives registration and the lefthand one prevents any skewing due to shrinkage, etc, of the cel.

you, so must be the base of the camera. This is a most important point.

An alternative arrangement, often illustrated in brochures of enlarger columns used for holding a camera for titling or copying, is to support the camera by its tripod socket on the end of an arm on the enlarger column. If you use this arrangement, the artwork must be upside down on the baseboard. Otherwise you will be filming it upside down.

Lighting

The lighting on the artwork must be reasonably even and—vitally important—must not cause reflections at the edges of the glass or cels. The standard arrangement is to have two lamps at approximately 45 degrees to the centre of the copyboard. In practice, problems of reflections will be minimized if the lamps are slightly lower than 45 degrees, say somewhere between 30 and 40 degrees. But they must not be so low that the lights cast shadows from the frame holding the glass.

The lamps must not be too close in or even illumination may be a problem. More important, lamps too close in will tend to give extra problems with reflections from the surface of the glass or of not-quite-flat cels. On the other hand, the lamps should not be unnecessarily far away or the light intensity may be too low to enable a moderate lens aperture to be used, rather than having the lens at, or near, fully open.

The intensity of light on the copyboard should be such that you will be working probably around $f4$ or even $f5.6$, where the lens performance will be about optimum and the depth of field will be great enough to cover any minor focusing errors. You will also probably use a 'normal' speed film, rather than ultra-fast, so in practice you will have a fairly rigid requirement for light level.

To some degree, the light intensity may have to be adjusted according to the size of the artwork to be lit. If you use very large artwork, you may have to settle for a somewhat lower level in order not to have unduly large lamps, or more likely at least two lamps on either side of the rostrum.

For most cartoon work, the artwork will be on cels or sheets of paper no larger than about 10×12 in (25×30 cm), and probably rather less than that, say A4 or perhaps 8×10 in. The photographed area will be appreciably smaller than the outside dimensions of the paper, as for ordinary titling. The register pins must be well outside the angle of view of the lens.

With this average size of cartoon artwork, the lamps can be something like 3 times the width of the area being filmed, away from the centre of the copyboard. This means that the lamps will probably be around 2 ft (6 m) away from the centre of the board.

Lamps

The choice of lamps can be narrowed immediately. The short-life photoflood type lamps are totally unsuitable for cartoon work. Suitable lamps would range from the 500 w 100 hour photographic types (nominally about 3200 K in colour temperature, or a shade less), down to 150 or 200 w household pearl bulbs.

Especially suitable for the more professional style of cartoon rostrum are the line-type tungsten-halogen studio lamps used in reflectors and designed to give an even spread of light. The longer life lamps should be used (say around 200 hour), and a pair of such lamps in the 1000 w size will easily illuminate a copyboard larger than the usual rather modest size used in cartooning.

Heat on the camera operator is a point to be watched. You do not want to be half roasted while you are filming, so a certain amount of screening or *barn doors* on the lamp units may be needed. The direct light of the lamps should also be screened from the camera.

Film

Most cartooning is on colour film. Indeed, black and white film is now so difficult to obtain that most people do not have the chance to use anything but colour.

The so-called Type A (indoor film) is used, since filming is normally with tungsten filament lamps. Professionals generally use Type B, designed for slightly lower colour temperature lamps than Type A which was originally designed for photofloods. In practice, both films seem well enough matched to the photographic type lamps not to need any additional filtration. Super 8 cameras, for example, may simply be set to the *filter out* (tungsten lamp) position, or the movielight key or screw fitted to the top of the camera to take out the filter.

When using household lamps with Type A film, this light may tend to be slightly too orange (too low colour temperature) in which case a *very* pale blue correction filter may be used over the camera lens. A glass B3 (30 Mired) filter is more than adequate, or a Wratten 82A (30 Mired) may be used; the latter can be in gelatin foil form, fixed over the front of the camera lens with adhesive tape. Take care not to put any finger marks on the filter.

Designing a rostrum

There is no difference in principle between a vertical titler, and a rostrum for cartoon filming. The layout can be basically identical, although the rostrum is probably a little more elaborate because it has register pins and most likely glass platen for holding the artwork flat.

Most cartoon makers begin by building their own rostrum. This is mainly because commercially available rostrums tend to be aimed well above the needs of the beginner though perhaps nicely aimed towards the semiprofessional and in particular the audiovisual producing users.

Happily, any home handyman can make a satisfactory rostrum for cartoon filming. Before settling the design, there are certain fundamental dimensions to be settled. First, there is the size of your artwork. Assuming you are working on sheets 8 × 10 in, A4 (8.25 × 11.7 in or 210 × 297 mm) or 10 × 12 in, your photographed area will be appreciably less than this, say around 6 × 8 in or 15 × 20 cm for the A4 sheet. The actual artwork will be somewhat larger than the photographed area so that you always have plenty of 'safety margin' when filming it and never run the risk of having the edge of the artwork in-picture.

Second, considering your particular camera, how best will it photograph this area? How close will its lens focus? If no closer than 5 ft (1.5 m), as with many lenses today, you may think this camera-to-artwork distance much too unwieldy a height for the rostrum for a simple fixed set-up. You can make it more compact by adding a supplementary lens to the camera.

Third, many professional rostrums have elaborate tracking arrangements for the camera to move up and down. For the beginner in cartooning, there is no need for this elaboration, particularly if you have a zoom lens on your camera since this can be used for zooming optically instead of moving the camera up or down, if you really must do a tracking shot.

Having settled your camera-to-copyboard distance, you can now decide the design and method of construction. Three alternative basic designs are:

(a) the single vertical strut at the back.
(b) the four-poster design.
(c) the excellent compromise, the braced single (or double) strut design.

The main point is that the camera support must be perfectly rigid. Bracing can be employed, as necessary, to avoid unduly heavy construction. The four-poster design is inherently rigid because it it self-braced. But the front posts tend to get in the way when changing cels—and that is something you have to do over and over again: specifically, some 18 or 24 times for every second of screen time. So a convenient-to-use layout is important.

Table movements

Professional rostrums often have a highly elaborate table, with movements east-west (for panning by moving the drawing while keeping the camera still), and also north-south for simulating camera movement. The simple home-made rostrum cannot have these elaborations, though they may, of course, be added later when you want more ambitious effects.

One feature you may well need, however, is the simpler one of a sideways movement of the *background* behind registered cels with the foreground action on them (usually something like a character walking). So here you have the foreground character on the cel(s) 'walking' on a fixed spot, and you move the background along frame-by-frame behind him. This always seems a wonderful effect when your see your efforts on the screen.

Professionally this is done by having the background mounted on the sideways-moving table, operated by lead-screws in between exposures of the single frames. The character is drawn on cels mounted on register pins mounted statically. So the background moves in a controlled way (so much per frame) behind the character. This can be done fairly easily without a moving-base table, simply by pulling the background picture slowly—in a guided straight line—sideways under the cel(s) with the character on them. To ensure smooth panning of the background, make marks along the edge to show how much it must be moved for each frame exposed. The total movement desired should be divided up into the number of frames to be shot on the scene, and the speed must 'match' that of the character's walking.

Drawing procedure

Generally you will find it best to draw *roughs* on plain white paper, thin enough to be reasonably translucent, yet absolutely firm because it has to be punched for fitting on the register pins. And it must withstand putting on to the pins and taking off again, several times.

If you stick one of your pin bars with adhesive tape (double-sided tape is excellent) to the opal top of an illuminated light-box you can trace through from the previous drawing, and so have the positioning correct for each new drawing relative to the previous one. You can then put on each new sheet of paper, with the already drawn previous frame's drawing underneath it, both accurately held on the register pins. As you draw the action of the new frame on the top sheet, you can see the positioning from the previous frame's drawing that is underneath. In this way, you will have the positioning correct for each new drawing, relative to the previous one.

In some cases, it is best to draw the start and finish positions of the action on separate sheets and then to do the in-between action in as many drawings as appropriate.

Always keep the drawing style *simple.* Reduce fussy detail to a minimum. Use bold lines and keep them the same in style from frame to frame.

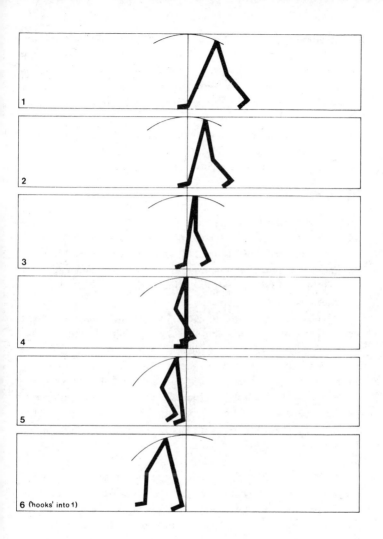

1

2

3

4

5

6 ('hooks' into 1)

A simple walking sequence showing basic leg movements and swing of the hips in an arc. In-between drawings can be made to smooth out the action.

If you study cartoon characters in television commercials you will see that the characters are almost always reduced in height to well below the natural proportions of humans. The average person is supposed to be around 7 or 8 'heads' high—that is, a person's height is about 7 or 8 times as great as the height of his head alone.

In cartooning, it is generally best to reduce this to give you a character perhaps 3 or 4 'heads' high—depending, naturally, on the character and the effect you want to produce.

Trying the effect

The simplest way to check the effect of your animation initially is to 'flip' the pile of successive drawings—like a child's flip-book. If you use moderately stiff paper for your roughs, this will facilitate 'flipping'. But the paper must be reasonably translucent, otherwise you will find it hard to see the picture underneath it on the light-box when drawing.

When you are doing the drawing on the light-box, you should mask off the opal around the sheets on which you are working. This will prevent glare. A typical light-box contains two 20w fluorescent lamps, with the neccessary control gear, in a white-lined box with a working top of 1/8 in (3 mm) thick opal *Perspex* or *Plexiglass*. If the box is large enough for the opal plastic to 'give' when you press on it, you can fix a sheet of plate glass about $\frac{1}{4}$ in (6 mm) thick, over the top, to act as the working surface. The pin bar is taped to the glass.

Once you have drawn a sequence or a scene that looks reasonable for animation when it is 'flipped', the beginner will find it worthwhile actually filming the roughs, to check exactly how the animation looks on the screen. The drawings can be taken on colour film, even though they are no more than black and white sketches.

Tracing

When you are satisfied with the roughs, you can proceed with the tracing—the operation in which the roughs are used as the basis for the finished drawings. For a simple job you might trace on the

Top A normal person is about seven heads high. Cartoon characters should usually be much less.
Bottom Exaggerated thin and plump characters, showing front and side dimensions.

light-box, on to plain white paper. Some notable prizewinning amateur cartoons have been made in this simple way.

For serious work, however, it is best to use the professionals' technique of tracing on to *cels*. These are simply sheets of cellulose acetate—like thin film-base—as sold in artists' materials shops.

For animation, you are obviously best advised to obtain cels ready cut to size, and there are several specialist firms who will supply animation film makers. Your immediate reaction to the bulk price will probably be surprise at the considerable expense of cartooning, as regards cel cost, for the price is generally stated per 1000 sheets. You may at first think you do not need so many, but if you use one cel per frame, you will need 3600 cels for a 50 ft roll of Super 8, or 4000 cels for a 100 ft roll of 16 mm. In this case your first pack of 1000 cels will not last you through one roll of film. In fact, you may use several cels at a time, for example one character on one cel, and a second character on another. The background, of course, will be separate, and can generally be on paper, under the cels.

If you use more than one cel at a time for some scenes, you should use the same total number of cels all through—even if blank cels are used. This is important in order to maintain the same 'quality' of picture throughout and especially from shot to shot. Professional animators never like to use more than four cels at a time because the larger number of cels tend to make the picture look oddly 'grey'.

You can often save artwork, and cels, by taking several frames of one cel. When there is no movement needed, you can perfectly well use the same cel over and over again, and this is normal practice in all cartoon studios.

The beginner may find it useful to shoot two frames of each cel, so halving the amount of drawing—but of course, at the expense of smoothness of movement. There is one very advanced Super 8 camera with microprocessor control that actually lets you select to expose 1, 2, 3 or 4 frames at each single press of the release.

The camera script

Animation shooting calls for careful planning and a carefully prepared working *camera script* to prevent mistakes.

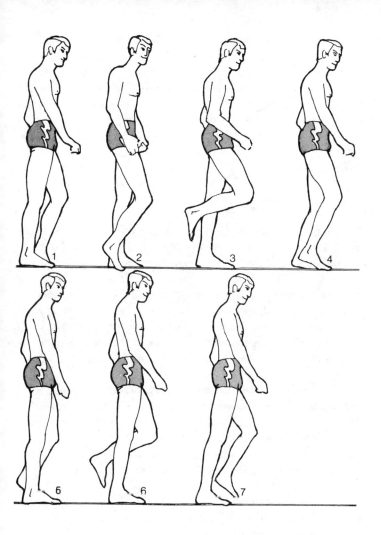

A walk sequence showing arm and body movement. Note that the right arm is forward when the left foot is forward.

Every drawing sheet should be numbered, and if several cels are to be combined they can be labelled A, B, C etc as well, to keep them in the same order in the pack. The numbering is especially important when two characters are on different cels and only one of them is moving (hence changing cels for every frame) while the other character holds still (same cel used for the prescribed number of frames). Numbering is also important when you have a cyclic action such as walking, where you can use the same cels for the repeating cycle.

Tracing methods

Normal practice for tracing from the rough on to the cel, is to put the rough on the pin bar on the drawing table (or the light box can be used) and then to put a new sheet of cel—also punched—on top of it. You then trace all the outlines from the rough, on to the cel. This is why the 'rough' must in fact be quite accurately drawn. Use drawing ink of the Indian ink type, and use a drafting pen that gives a particular line thickness. The line thickness should be quite appreciable and, depending on the size of the artwork, you will need a pen giving a line somewhere between 0.5 mm and 1.0 mm wide.

Trace the outline *on the top surface of the cel.* When all the cels of the scene or sequence have been traced, you can then proceed to the next stage, which is *filling in with colour on the back.* Fill in the outlines of the character with colour, which is generally poster paint. Some firms have made special paints for cels, designed to go on very smoothly and not to crack or peel off easily. However, such paints no longer seem to be generally available. You simply put in areas of flat colour, and no attempt is made to have any shading on individual frames. Indeed, the task is to keep a perfect consistency of colour through the film.

To achieve the best frame-by-frame consistency, you should *paint all of one colour area on all the cels, in sequence.* Then go back to the first cel and start another colour, and paint that all through. And so on. If you try to finish one cel at a time with all its colours, you will almost invariably find you have a surprising amount of colour 'flicker' in the finished film.

Remember you fill in only the outlines of the character on the cell. The surrounding area is left clear. Thus, when the cel is super-imposed on the background for filming, the character on the cel appears superimposed on the background.

Hints on drawing

Some flair for drawing is needed for an elaborate animated cartoon, but it is suprising how effective very simple drawings can be when you give them the magic of animation. It is far better—easier, too—to draw funny little rounded characters, than to attempt represent-ations of real people.

Remember the stunted proportions, the large face on short fat body, that look so right when animated. Study the television commercials that use animation; they contain many exciting ideas. Expressions can be very simply achieved with relatively few lines (*see* p. 179), and as a beginning project you might consider doing a sequence of these expressions, filling in the intermediate frames as one expression changes to another. You can adapt the expressions into the face of one of the other cartoon characters or, better still, one of your own making.

Movement, especially walking, is always a challenge. The simplest walking cycle might use four positions, but this would look quite jerky and a six-position walk is perhaps the least you should use. You can try this out very easily by tracing from illustrations (*see* p. 187).

Titling for Slides

Good titling technique is just as important in slides as it traditionally is in cine. There are two types of title slide. First is the 'pure' title, which you can—and indeed should—use for your home slide shows. It will certainly add a satisfying professional touch, for using starting titles and an end title helps to round off even a simple personal slide show.

Second is the audiovisual area, the slide of a graph, chart or other informational material, which is usually part of a lecture. Sometimes slides are used, and other times the so-called overhead projector transparencies. The important point with either medium is legibility on the screen—a point all too often ignored.

Sizes and proportions

When people talk about slides nowadays, they usually mean 24 × 36 mm *(full-frame)* colour transparencies. The first point to note is the proportions: 3:2, which is very different from the 4:3 of standard format movies. The mount size for these so-called 35 mm slides is 50 × 50 mm (approx 2 × 2 in).

One thing must be said at the outset: these slide pictures can be of either horizontal or vertical format. Some people have square screens, so they can project either shape without problems. But many slides have to be projected on cine screens—in lecture theatres, for example—and it is therefore desirable in many cases to make 2:2 slides exclusively in the horizontal format.

Other formats

Within the 50 × 50 mm (2 × 2 in) overall size of slide, several other mask dimensions are available from various manufacturers, for example:

24×18 mm   (half-frame)

24×24 mm   (square format on 35 mm film)

28×28 mm   (Instamatic 126-size)

40×40 mm   (the so-called Superslide)

Note that except for half-frame, each of these is a square format.

Then there are the larger format slides, using 6×6 cm ($2\frac{1}{4} \times 2\frac{1}{4}$ in) transparencies, again square, and these are generally in 7×7 cm mounts. A more recent variation in this slide size is the addition of the 16-on and 15-on 120 film format which is $6 \times 4\frac{1}{2}$ in.

Traditional 'lantern slide' sizes, less and less used today, are $3\frac{1}{4} \times 3\frac{1}{4}$ in (Britain) and $3\frac{1}{4} \times 4$ in (USA).

Except for the last two sizes, the various slide sizes are based on the popular camera films, and can be made on reversal type colour film or by conventional darkroom techniques with black and white films.

Cameras for slide making

As with cine titles, it is desirable to use a through-the-lens reflex camera when doing any close-up photography such as slide-making. The 35 mm SLR is now so widely used that this is the type of camera likely to be available. The 35 mm full-frame format is the most popular today, both in the home and in virtually all lecture theatres. The basic advantage of a reflex camera is that it lets you see what you will be taking, right up to the moment of exposure.

It is quite possible—though less practical—to use a non-reflex camera for taking slides. You can use a supplementary close-up lens (*see* p. 26) on a still camera, just as with cine. For example, you can use a +2 dioptre supplementary and place the camera at $\frac{1}{2}$ m ($19\frac{1}{2}$ in) from the original being photographed. The lens is set to infinity, and the distance measured from the supplementary to the title or other original being photographed. You can also use the focusing adjustment of the lens if you need to move in closer (*see* Tables on p. 26–27).

You can use a supplementary lens with an SLR, too, in the event that the lens will not focus close enough to cope with small originals. And with the SLR you can focus visually. You will find a +1 dioptre (No 1) supplementary very useful when using an SLR for copy work.

Most 35 mm cameras, even the non-SLR models, have one great advantage over most cine cameras: you can open the camera back, hold the shutter open by using the B setting with a lock-on cable release, and study the image by placing a piece of tracing paper—or, better, ground glass—across the film plane. By using this trick, you can easily set up even a non reflex model—providing it is not one of the early models such as the Leica II or III of revered memory, without a hinged back.

Viewfinder accuracy

For slides, you must have exactly the correct framing when the film is inserted in the slide-mount for projection. So viewfinder accuracy is very important—far more so in title making than in most ordinary picture-taking.

You should check your camera before doing any important slides, and you can do this by comparing the viewfinder image with what you see on tracing paper or ground glass held or taped across the camera gate. You may need to keep off extraneous light by viewing the image under a dark cloth, like an old-time photographer studying his ground glass.

Another way to check the viewfinder on an SLR is simply to photograph a suitable chart—a newspaper pinned up on the wall would do—and to note carefully the picture limits in the viewfinder on all four sides.

It is helpful if you have an assistant to mark the picture limits you can see in the viewfinder, using a felt-tip pen boldly to mark your chart or sheet of newspaper, at your direction.

Expose a negative (or transparency, if you prefer) of this chart, and after processing mount it in a slide and project it. With many otherwise excellent SLRs, you will be surprised if not shocked at the lack of accuracy in your viewfinder. You must make allowance for the inaccuracy of your particular camera when setting up any titles.

196

This inaccuracy is of two types. First is the so-called *safety margin,* where you get more all around on the film than you saw in the viewfinder. Some cameras show as much as 18 per cent more of picture width and height, on the film, than was seen in the viewfinder. Many cameras aim for a 5 per cent error, while some manufacturers (eg: Nikon) say they aim for a dead cut, based on the standard slide-mount size.

A slight difficulty arises here because the standard slide-mount mask size is less than the full nominal 24×36 mm of the image recorded on the film. It has to be, otherwise the edges of the picture would be shown on the screen.

The second form of viewfinder inaccuracy is simple off-centre placement, and this too is something you will immediately see if you make a test as described. Off-centre finder image happens less on still cameras than on cine, due to the larger size of the still frame, which makes it easier to engineer and set up more accurately. But users often find sufficient off-centre effect to spoil the line-up of title slides with borders around the wording.

Lenses and distances

The standard lens is perfectly satisfactory for slides of titles and charts. With 35 mm SLRs, this lens is generally about 50 or 55 mm focal length, and such lenses are usually outstandingly well corrected nowadays and will give excellent sharpness to the edges of lines all over the picture field. Copy material such as charts and tables will be excellently reproduced.

If you need to photograph extremely small charts, approaching same-size, the average standard lens does not perform so well and a special *macro* or *micro* lens should be used. This has a simpler optical construction and smaller maximum aperture than the ordinary standard lens, and has a coarse focusing thread that will go down to, typically, half-size. That is, it will photograph a subject down to about 3 in wide, reducing it to the (approximately) 1½ in wide negative size, and fills the width of the 35 mm gate. More accurately, it can reduce a subject as little as 72 mm wide, down to the 36 mm on the negative. The slide mount aperture is normally approximately 34.5 mm wide.

If you wish to photograph subjects down to 1:1 (same-size), the special macro or micro lenses generally have a special extension ring which you place between the lens and the camera body. Those who are likely to have to buy a macro lens specially for work of this nature should consider one with a focal length about double that of the standard lens, which helps to keep the camera at a sufficient distance away from the subject to permit easier lighting without shadows of the camera lens and other encumberances.

The average 35 mm SLR 50 mm standard lens will focus down to around $\frac{1}{2}$ m (500 mm or about 20 in). This means it will go down approximately to a 10:1 reduction of the subject width on to the film. Since the film image is roughly $1\frac{1}{2}$ in wide, the smallest title card or chart you can photograph without a supplementary lens or an extension tube is about 15 in wide. So, for almost all practical title and chart photography, you will need either a supplementary lens or an extension tube.

It is easy to calculate the lens-to-film distance for any given title size (actual photographed width). The size of the full-frame slide aperture is normally approximately 34.5 mm wide and 22.5 mm high.

Remember the basic rule of optics: reduction ratio is the same as the ratio of

$$\frac{\text{lens-to-film distance}}{\text{subject-to-film distance}}$$

Thus, a 9 in wide title photographed area reduced down to the 35 mm width of approximately $1\frac{1}{2}$ in is a 6:1 reduction. The title-to-lens distance will be six times the lens-to-film distance. With a 50 mm (approximately 2 in) lens, and allowing for a little extension of the lens for the fairly close focusing, we can say a lens-to-film distance of about 2.2 in, and hence a lens-to-title distance of 6 times that, or 13.2 in. Nowadays you will probably work out the distance in metric dimensions, and this may sound a little more complicated but most people use a calculator.

More accurately, you can calculate the lens-to-film distance and

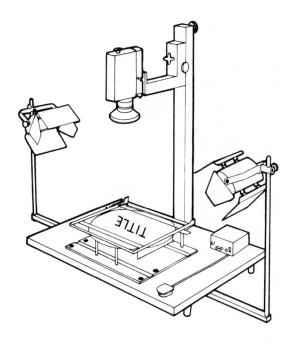

The Oxberry Pro-Copy F2 titling/animation unit. The same unit is also widely used with a still camera for slide-making.

the title-to-film distance, very simply by applying these formulae.

lens-to-film distance

$$=f(1+\frac{1}{r})$$

where f=focal length of camera lens
and r=reduction ratio

title-to-lens distance
$$=f(1+r)$$

Example: 55 mm lens, title area 200 mm wide, to be reduced to 34.5 mm frame width of slide mount. Reduction is

$$\frac{34.5}{200}=0.17 \text{ (approx) which is } \frac{1}{5.9}.$$

Then lens-to-film distance

$$=f(1+\frac{1}{r})=55(1+\frac{1}{5.9})=55(1+0.17)$$

$$=55\times1.17=64.35 \text{ mm}.$$

And lens-to-title distance

$$=f(1+r)=55(1+5.9)=55(6.9)$$

$$=379.5 \text{ mm (15 in)}.$$

Note: *always use the same units throughout the calculation.*

Camera set-ups

Just as with cine titling, you can make slides with either a horizontal set-up or a vertical one. Simplest of all for taking the odd title slide is perhaps to pin the title card to the wall and set up the camera on a tripod lined up square with the title. Using a reflex, you can see to frame and focus.

It is quite feasible to use a couple of lamps, each aimed at about 45 degrees to the title, and at a sufficient distance away to give even illumination and no risk of reflections on the card.

A still camera has a standard lens about half the respective focal length for the format size. So a still camera lens takes in a much wider angle at a given distance. For this reason, it is often better to use a longer lens than standard on the still camera, to keep the camera far enough away from the title for the lights to shine on it without any obstructions. Thus on a 35 mm SLR, it may be more convenient to use say an 85 mm, or perhaps a 100 or 105 mm, even though these longer lenses are not usually as well corrected as the standard lens.

If your title is a chart with borders which must appear true, take care to keep the camera lens centred with the title, in both directions. Any slight lack of centring will tend to show a little less when you are using a longer focal length lens but lack of squareness seems to show up rather badly on the screen, and is a sign of careless lining-up.

There is no reason why you should not construct a simple title bench if you plan to do much slide-making. The horizontal titlers for cine (see p. 83) will give ideas on construction.

While the horizontal set-up is often the more versatile, a vertical arrangement is most convenient, especially if you have a good firm tripod that will let you locate the title card between two of the legs, and point the camera vertically down to the centre of the title. Lights can be shone in at an angle that just avoids throwing shadows of the tripod legs on the title area. The vertical camera is particularly convenient for looking into the viewfinder, as long as the camera can be kept at a convenient height. Sometimes this may mean using the standard lens for a larger title card and a longer lens when taking a smaller title card, thus keeping the camera at about the same height.

Some ordinary enlargers allow the head to be removed and replaced with a platform or a complete new arm with a camera platform on it. This is a convenient arrangement, especially if the enlarger has a moderately long column. To bring the camera to about the right height for looking down into the finder eyepiece, the enlarger may be placed on the floor, and lamps arranged to shine down on to the baseboard. An alternative is to add a right-angle viewfinder eyepiece, and to leave the enlarger at bench height.

For anyone who plans to do a lot of slide-making, a vertical titling stand can be built from wood or slotted angle. The cartoon 'rostrum' (see p. 199) will give ideas here.

For the professional audio-visual studio, one of the big motion picture rostrum companies, Oxberry, offer a range of titling stands for still and cine, and these give great convenience.

Film for slides

Most slides will be taken on colour reversal film. In general, the slower films are preferable to the fast ones, because the slower the film, the finer the grain and the better the definition.

With colour film, you have a choice using daylight or artificial light film, with most makes. It is easiest to use the film that is matched to the type of light you will be using.

Almost invariably it is best to use artificial light, and the 100-hour type 3200K photopearl lamps are generally very convenient if you have reflectors with ES lampholders. A pair of such lamps in reflectors will serve for most title slide making.

The colour difference between these Type B (3200K) photopearl lamps, and the very slightly 'bluer' photofloods, is negligible on title subjects. Photofloods are not so desirable because of their much shorter and highly unpredictable life.

If you use daylight film with tungsten filament lamps of these types, you will need to add an 80A filter over the lens (for 3200K lamps), or an 80B for photofloods. The filter is blue and has an exposure increase factor of approximately 4 times. If you use the camera's internal through-the-lens metering, take the reading through the filter and this will be near enough allow for the filter factor.

If you use tungsten type film in daylight, use an 85 filter over the lens. This has an exposure increase factor of about $\frac{2}{3}$ of an f stop. Again the internal metering would allow for it, within practical limits.

Using black and white

You can shoot black and white originals on colour film, normally, of course, colour reversal for slide making. However, if you have your own darkroom facilities, it is generally more convenient, and more economical, to use black and white stock and to do your own processing.

While colour slides virtually *have* to be reversal, in the case of

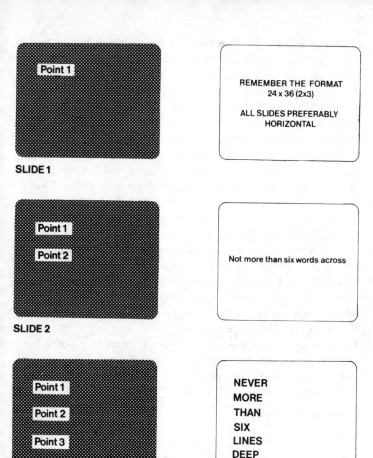

Slide-making: Adding successive points to the artwork, taking a new slide (in register) for each addition. Project one after the other during the lecture as each new point arises.

black and white it is often better to project the negative. In this way, you obtain white lettering on a black ground, which tends to show less glare on the screen.

The best film for making this type of slide from line originals is one of the *microfilm* type materials. These give incredibly good definition, far exceeding that of ordinary camera films, and a smoothness of image that is a delight to see. The microfilm materials are normally supplied unperforated, so you must be sure to order *perforated* 35 mm. They are generally sold in 100 ft lengths, so you have to load your own cassettes—in the dark since the film is panchromatic. The main suppliers insist on fairly large bulk orders, but there are various sub-suppliers who are prepared to sell one 100 ft roll at a time. Microfilm is fairly slow and around 6 ASA is a good starting point for exposure tests. Since the emulsion is high contrast, exposure is very critical indeed, and certainly has to be within half a stop. The density of the 'black' should be no more than a dark grey, since these films are designed for optimum performance without having to give really dense blacks, as was the case with older microfilm materials.

For processing microfilm, you can use a normal print developer and, if you standardize your time and temperature (eg: 4 min at 20C), you will obtain consistent results of startlingly good quality.

Title cards for slides

You can use any of the title lettering systems already described for cine titles, and the title area will then depend on the size of the lettering being used. If you make title cards with one of the lettering systems such as Letraset, it is a good idea to standardize the title card size at the professionally adopted 10 × 12 in (or 250 × 300 mm). It is also useful to standardize the size of the photographed area on the card. This should be central, so that you can line up each card automatically on the title bench by placing one corner of the card into an L-shaped locating piece screwed to the bench (or fixed with double-sided tape).

When preparing title cards for the standard full-frame 35 mm format with proportions of 2 high:3 wide, you can have a photographed area 10 in wide and approx 7 in high. The title wording should lie well inside that, say within an area 9 in wide and 6 in high, at the most.

Type size

The size of lettering on the screen that can be read at the maximum viewing distance (usually the back of the room) by a person with normal eyesight, can be defined in terms of the viewing distance and the screen size. For slides, it is usual to talk in terms of screen *height*, to cope with square formats as well as rectangular, the latter being arranged horizontally. This does not take into account that the rectangular slides are sometimes shown vertically; as stated earlier, this is not a preferred practice for many lecture halls. A widely accepted practice for slide projection is that the maximum viewing distance should be not more than 8 times the screen height. Thus, a lecture room with the back row of seats 48 ft from the screen should have a screen at least 6 ft high. The lettering height should never be smaller than $\frac{1}{50}$ of the screen height and preferably larger than that, say $\frac{1}{25}$ of screen height. Based on the suggested artwork photographed area of 6 in high, this means that the smallest letter size will be $\frac{1}{8}$ in high (giving $\frac{1}{48}$ of screen height), with a preference for lettering $\frac{1}{4}$ in (6 mm) high ($\frac{1}{24}$ of screen height), or possibly 0.2 in, giving $\frac{1}{30}$ H.

It is worthwhile to make a test title card with various sizes of lettering on it, and to photograph and project it as a slide in some typical lecture rooms—or at home, if your slides are destined for home consumption. It is surprising how quickly small lettering becomes unreadable as one moves back from the front row.

It does not matter whether the projection is of a 2×2 in slide, or a slide on $2\frac{1}{4}$ in square film, or even a 10×10 in overhead projector transparency. The rule about minimum lettering size applies equally to all slide formats.

In the case or artwork for charts and tables, there are often lines to be ruled for columns and borders. The line width should be not less than 100 times the screen height. The exact width will depend on the proportions of the artwork lettering. Ink pens for drawing lines can be selected accordingly.

Since many slides are made on colour film, it is usual to do the artwork on coloured paper or card. For example, white lettering on a rich blue background looks extremely good.

Selection of typefaces for good legibility is important for slides, as for cine (*see* p. 36). In the event that there is much type to be 'set' on the artwork by relatively unskilled lettering artists, even with the press-down type systems such as Letraset, Prestype, Deca-Dry, etc, it may be advisable to use larger type and a larger title card, so working to a greater reduction in the photography. For example, one professional audiovisual unit works with originals at 10 times size and a nominal 240×360 mm photographed area, which fits neatly on a half-sheet of *Color-Aid* coloured background paper.

Hints for informational slides

When planning slides of charts, graphs, etc, remember that the illustration in the average printed paper from a journal will not be optimum for slides. Slides should contain a minimum of detail and reading matter. Where lettering is essential, it should be large and bold. When not essential, it should be left out. Any details can, after all, be explained orally.

Tables of figures are rarely suitable for slides. If absolutely essential, they should be restricted to no more than about five columns of up to five entries each.

Graph paper does not normally reproduce well on a slide and should not be used. Only a few grid lines need be shown, and these can be drawn. Engineering drawings hardly ever reproduce well on slides, since they are too detailed. They should be redrawn using bold lines and lettering.

Informational slides can be built up as a sequence, adding one extra line of wording on each successive slide, for example.

A good general guide to sizes which uses widely available materials is suggested in the British Standard. Here the paper or card size is A4 (210×297 mm). A transparent grid may be used for placing the desired wording in the following areas:

Maximum photographed area: 165×230 mm, giving $6\frac{2}{3}$ reduction on to the film.

Safe area for wording: 150×215 mm.

Note that no borders should be drawn on master copy. All the artwork should be drawn into the *horizontal* 3×2 format layout.

Letter size: smallest 4 mm (1/40H)

intermediate 5 mm (1/33H)

main lettering and figures (1/27H)

Line thickness: thin—eg: grid lines on chart approx. 0.4 mm (1/400H)

medium—eg: axis lines on graph approx. 0.8 mm (1/200H)

thick—eg: graph data lines approx. 1.5 mm (1/100H)

Overhead projectors

A rather special and widely used form of projector for transparencies is the *overhead projector* (OHP). This generally uses 10×10 in transparencies, which can be mounted into a cardboard mount for easier handling, though the mount is not essential since the transparency is simply laid on the horizontal glass top. Below this glass top is the lamphouse, typically with a 650 w lamp, and there is a simple condenser system—usually a Fresnel type moulded in plastic—just under the glass top. Above this is the projection lens with an adjustable mirror (surface silvered) that turns the beam forwards on to the screen.

Initially the OHP began life as a very modern sort of 'blackboard' for teaching purposes. The 10×10 in format is large enough to permit writing and drawing directly on to a plain cel laid on the glass top. This is the reason for using such a large format. This same factor has the advantage of outstandingly good light efficiency, so that the OHP can be used in a not very well darkened room.

The basic idea of the OHP is that the lecturer uses it from a position in front of the audience. For this reason, the focal length of the projection lens has to be extremely short, to project a very large picture from a very short throw. A typical OHP operates on a projection distance of approximately $1\frac{1}{3}$ times the width of the picture it is throwing. Different models vary somewhat but this is a good basis on which to study projection conditions.

To fill a 6 ft (1.85 m) high screen, the typical projection distance will be about 8 ft between projector and screen. If you cannot place the projector this far away, the picture will not fill the screen and you will need to use larger lettering if it is to remain readable for viewers further back.

As a practical rule, with optimum projection conditions, you should not use any lettering smaller than $\frac{1}{4}$ in high (1/40 of picture height) on overhead projector transparencies. There is no difference in the rules for size of lettering on the screen for good legibility, whether using slides or OHP transparencies. The basic problem with the OHP is that it is generally placed too close to the screen because the lecturer wishes to keep clear of the front row of seats. In this case, larger lettering is called for on the original.

It is hardly practical, for reasons of cost, to make OHP transparencies by conventional photographic methods. Some companies with full process-camera facilities think nothing of taking a 10 × 12 in sheet of lith film and photographing a chart by conventional line-negative making methods. The results, as would be expected, are excellent but to work on 2 × 2 in slides is infinitely more economical.

The original concept of the OHP was that you drew your own slides or wording directly on to plain cels. But the need has arisen to make transparencies from more professionally prepared original material such as typing for charts and similar data. This can in effect be *contact printed* onto a transparent copy material.

Copying machines for OHP transparencies

The simplest type of copying machine for making OHP 'slides' by contact printing is the thermal or infra-red copier. These are made by a number of manufacturers, of whom the 3M Company is perhaps the best known. They are very simple to use and the special film is not unduly expensive, at least not compared with conventional photographic film.

With these machines, the original is placed in contact with a sheet of the special heat-film, and the pair are fed into the mouth of the unit and transported through by rollers, past the infra-red bar which effects the 'printing', and out again.

The speed of the transport rollers can be adjusted to control the 'exposure', and hence the density of the printed transparency.

The special thermal film is available in several types from various manufacturers. The usual type is *direct reversal*—that is, a black-on-white original will copy as black lettering on white ground. Other versions are made giving coloured lettering on white (transparent) ground. Negative working film is also available, and this gives clear lettering on black background (or in some cases a coloured background), from the usual original which is written or typed on white paper.

Some office copying machine systems, Xerox for example, offer a film type material for making OHP transparencies instead of paper copies as is usual. These systems are not always well publicized, but they work extremely well if you have the appropriate copying machine.

Originals for OHPs

As long as you have a copying machine of one of the types described, it is always easier to write or draw your title or chart on paper, rather than directly on to cel (acetate). So various possibilities have become practical.

The most important is typewriting, though this is almost always too small to give good or even reasonable legibility to most of the audience. However, there are available special typewriters with giant type, specially designed for making OHP title originals. Any company intending to use their OHP frequently for training or presentation of information would do well to consider purchasing one of these special typewriters. Users of certain Golfball typewriters can obtain a special large-type golfball, made with OHP use in mind. The ordinary Pica—or worse, the smaller Elite—typewriter type is much too small for most OHP work, and if used it will be readable only by the front few rows of audience.

One ingenious, but misguided, photographer had the bright idea of photographing the typed copy on to microfilm in a 35 mm camera, then enlarging this on to bromide paper to give a print about 3 times the size of the typing. He intended to copy this on a thermal copier to make the OHP transparency. It would have been easier and more economical to use the 35 mm negative as a 2 × 2 in slide!

Layout of originals for OHP use

The most important advice—just as for 35 mm slides—is not to try and put too much into one slide. The fact that you can easily use a full page of typing as an original for OHP use, either on a 10 × 10 in or A4 format overhead projector, is no excuse for doing it. It is best to take no more typing than would fill half or perhaps just one-third of a normal page and, by retyping on a large typewriter, perhaps, to fill the OHP frame with that.

Other possibilities are to use lettering such as Letraset, and special types are made that will withstand the warmth in the OHP thermal copier. Be sure to use this special sort of lettering. Less exotic, perhaps, is to use Indian ink stencils of the *Uno* and similar types. At worst, you can do some neat writing in Indian ink, or with a thicker type of felt-tip pen, and copy that. It is better to use a handwritten transparency that the audience can read, than a neatly typed one that they cannot.

Remember the opportunity for adding colours to the OHP transparency. There are sets of special transparent inks and felt-tipped pens available for this purpose. Carefully used, they can give very good looking transparencies. Normally they are used in addition to the prepared or thermal printed black lines on the transparency.

Index